Creating Organizational Soul

The Source of Positive Change and Transformation

Richard Bellingham, Ed.D.

HRD Press, Inc. • Amherst • Massachusetts

Published by: HRD Press, Inc.
22 Amherst Road
Amherst, MA 01002
800-822-2801 (U.S. and Canada)
413-253-3488
413-253-3490 (fax)
www.hrdpress.com

ISBN 978-1-59996-189-7

Production services by Jean Miller
Cover design by Eileen Klockars
Editorial services by Suzanne Bay

— Contents —

Part 6: The Pragmatics
Chapter 8: What are the Conditions and Standards

— Preface —

Who would have the nerve to write a book about organizational soul? Believe me, I understand that this undertaking is unabashedly pretentious. It took surviving Vietnam, the Pentagon, jails, drug rehab, teen-age pregnancy, the educational system, the health care system, homelessness, the Canadian Mounties, and corporate America before I figured out that I had survived so many soul-threatening experiences that I needed to write about them. I hope that through this book I can make some contribution toward changing the experience for those who come after me.

Here's the short story: I was born and raised in an all-white community a few miles north of Kalamazoo, Michigan (yes, there really is a Kalamazoo). There were no African Americans, no Hispanics, no Asians, and no gays that anyone knew about. There was almost no crime, and even fewer divorces. Child and sexual abuse were secrets no one talked about.

Like 99% of all the students from our school who decided to apply to college, I never looked outside a radius of 50 miles from home. I couldn't have named any of the ivy league schools or told you where they were located on a bet. Unlike my peers in New York, I didn't have the faintest idea of acceptance rates or requirements at any school outside of Michigan.

Things went swimmingly well for me all through my four years at Western Michigan University: Fraternity president, chairman of the Disciplinary Committee, president of the Honor Society, blah, blah, blah. Oh, things looked very promising for me: blond, built, blue eyes, good looking—all the preferred presenting variables of the time. I simply had the misfortune of graduating in 1967 at the peak of the Vietnam draft. Everything changed.

It was Fort Knox and a buzz cut. It was Fort Holabird, spy training, and invading Fort Lauderdale from a submarine. It was Vietnam for a year. Everything changed.

I managed to survive Saigon for a year in civilian clothes and check out all the French restaurants. Listening to bullets whistling over my head on guard duty from 2:00 a.m. to 4:00 a.m. kept the adrenaline flowing enough to digest all the fine food. I saw U.S. soldiers go out of their way to splash lovely Asian women dressed in their white, flowing dresses. I saw young, once-robust GIs in field hospitals with their legs or arms blown off and their lives wasted. I attended the funeral service for a good friend who got caught in sniper fire. I saw soldiers demonizing all Vietnamese as gooks. I witnessed de-humanization on a mass scale. Day after day. *Everything changed.*

I came home to an America that did not view me as a war hero. The overriding perception was that our participation in the war meant that we supported it. The public didn't want to hear about what we had been through. I didn't want to talk about it. I joined Vietnam Veterans Against the War and participated in protest marches. *Everything changed.*

And that's why I have the nerve to write a book about organizational soul. Forty years late, maybe, but then again, I gained a perspective from my struggles over the past 40 years that I did not have at age 25. And things have not exactly improved.

During my time as a recovering Vietnam vet, I have worked with over 200 organizations worldwide. I have experienced the gracious hospitality of Santiago, Chile. I have visited companies in India that have meditation rooms as integral components of their facilities. I have worked with organizations in China, Hong Kong, Singapore, Korea, and Japan. I have facilitated retreats in Germany, France, Spain, and England. I've worked with leaders in most of the Fortune 100 companies and with scores of mom-and-pop shops. I've met soulless leaders, but many more others who are soulful.

While I have had the good fortune to work in most corners of the world, some of my most satisfying professional experiences have come from doing pro-bono work for local not-for-profit organizations. I have worked with the Somerset Hills YMCA for the past 25 years in capacities ranging from board chairman to strategic planning consultant. I have also had the pleasure of working with Homeless Solutions for the past 15 years, helping with board development, staff development, and strategic planning, and was privileged to help the Visiting Nurse Association of Somerset Hills, a wonderfully soulful organization.

I'm writing this book to share what I have learned from all these experiences in the hope that more organizations will strive diligently to develop an organizational soul.

— Introduction —

Soul is normally thought about from an individual point of view in the context of a person's individual quest to develop his or her essential self. Some see creating soul as the goal of religion. Others see it as the result of spiritual growth. Plato defined soul as the source of all change and transformation. Plotinus defined it as the beginning of all things. The great psychologist Carl Jung defined soul as the source of our enthusiasm and inspiration.

This book explores the importance of soul as a creative force in organizations. While I do not suggest that there is any religious significance to organizational soul, I do believe that organizational soul influences work spirit or *esprit de corps.* Indeed, in this book, a case is made for the strong connection between organizational soul and productivity, innovation, and results. Clearly, creating organizational soul and achieving the resultant outcomes requires leadership.

A wise friend of mine once said, "Leadership is about getting people to want to do what they need to do." This book is about getting people and organizations to want to do what they need to do in order to create organizational soul and achieve extraordinary results. There is certainly plenty of evidence that we need to do something differently.

It's 2009—almost the end of the first decade in the new millennium. The economy is crumbling. The earth is in peril. People are starving. We are still killing each other—and getting better at it. The gap between rich and poor continues to widen. The trend lines are heading in the wrong direction. America, the ultimate consumer society, is staggering under unprecedented debt. Our savings rate has declined from 11% to -1%

over the past 20 years. Home prices are falling. Foreclosure rates are skyrocketing. Our credit card debt just passed the trillion-dollar threshold. The lowest income group in America spends almost 10% of its income on lottery tickets. Asian and European countries are funding our spending habits by lending us money so we can buy their goods. Credit is tightening. Jobs are hard to come by. Our educational achievement scores are declining and we are falling further behind other countries. We have slashed funding for basic research. So where's the good news?

First and foremost, you picked up this book. The notion of creating organizational soul peaked your curiosity and intrigued you enough to explore the possibilities. The idea of creating positive change and transformation led you to take action.

You are not alone. Several organizations are stepping up to the challenge and seeking positive change and transformation. Hundreds of small groups are advocating for the environment. Lots of organizations mobilize efforts to provide food aid. Some groups are dedicated to finding and eliminating land mines. On a less dramatic scale, many businesses, social service agencies, and educational institutions are looking for ways to create a green, safe, humane, and peaceful world.

Individual character is forged in the mills of adversity. Jeffery Sachs, director of the Earth Institute at Columbia University and special advisor to the United Nations, is creating new economic models to save communities from starving. Paul Farmer, the founder of Partners in Health and a professor of Medical Anthropology at Harvard University, created clinics in Haiti, Russia, Rwanda, Lesotho, Malawi, and Peru to provide free medical treatment to poor people. Greg Mortensen, the author of the best-selling *Three Cups of Tea,* is building schools in Pakistan and Afghanistan to provide thinking alternatives to the madrassas' brainwashing techniques. Bob Carkhuff, the founder of Possibilities Communities, is generating interdependent economic models that create endless possibilities for people in all aspects of society. No matter how bleak the environment and conditions, there is always the possibility of an exemplary leader stepping up and making a difference. Lucy Calkins, director of the Reading and Writing Project at Columbia Teacher's College, is developing models to improve literacy among under-served populations. Julie Meek, the CEO of an innovative health services company, is creating health-care models that not only help people feel and function better, but also reduce health-care costs. Betsey Hall, the CEO of Homeless Solutions, is providing care and support for people to become self-reliant. Dean Furbush, president of College Summit, is helping urban youth get a college education. No matter how bleak the environment and conditions, there is always the possibility of an exemplary individual or organization stepping up and making a difference.

We still have a chance of turning this around. But it will take soul—soul that can only come when people work collaboratively for a larger purpose, shaped by humility and inquiry and motivated by love and justice.

The intent of this book is to take a hard look at where we are and look for ways to get better. As Victor Frankl suggested in *The Man's Search for Ultimate Meaning*, the key to meaning in life is to see the possibilities against the backdrop of our current reality. The search for meaning can apply to organizations, as well as to individuals.

To me, getting better means "moving up the scales." This book contains many scales that will help you track progress in your life and in your organization. In each moment, we have a choice of how we act. We can be a leader, a contributor, a participant, an observer, or a detractor. This range of behaviors can be captured in the following scale:

Leader
Contributor
Participant
Observer
Detractor

We know from history that human behavior ranges from better to worse. There are heinous examples of large-scale unimaginable evil (e.g. the Holocaust, ethnic cleansing, famine, genocide) and there are inspiring examples of unimaginable good (the American Revolution, Oscar Schindler, Mother Theresa, Nelson Mandela). Courageous leaders step up and make a difference. They have real *soul*. The extent to which their impact takes hold depends upon the soul of the organization. It is either fertile and nurturing, or cold and hard. This book is about creating conditions in which courageous leadership can have *sustainable* impact.

Yes, this book is about creating organizational soul in our schools, in our community agencies, and in our corporations— not because it would be a nice thing to do, but because it is necessary for our survival and growth.

Part 1:

The Path

The pleasure of the soul appears to be found in the journey of discovery, the unfolding revelation of expanded insight and experience.

— Anthony Lawlor

–1–

My 40-Year Search for Soul

M y search for corporate soul began when I landed in a county jail 40 years ago. I had just returned from a tour of duty with Army intelligence in Vietnam, terribly disillusioned by the dehumanization I had experienced and observed in the streets of Saigon, and had taken a job as the director of Rehabilitation for the Kalamazoo County Jail. I had a staff of 14 people working in the basement of the jail, helping inmates improve their level of physical, emotional, and intellectual functioning. We found corporations that would take a risk on some of our "graduates" and hire them for entry-level jobs. Those corporations had enough soul to hire individuals who might have stolen from them directly or indirectly in the past. They knew that unless something was done, many of these same people would steal from them in the future. We linked inmates up with the social service agencies that could help them make the transition back to society. Together, we reduced recidivism by 50% over a three-year time period based on re-arrest (the most stringent definition of recidivism). These results set the national standard for inmate rehabilitation. When an organization looks beyond itself, invests in its community, and believes in possibilities, it is not only doing the right thing—it is also achieving great results for itself and for its community. And it presents a compelling rationale for creating corporate soul.

What does it take to create organizational soul? Successful inmate rehabilitation and organizational transformation are remarkably similar, as you will soon discover.

One component of our comprehensive solution to prevent recidivism was to offer the inmates a wide array of programming. We established a mobile book store, taught high school equivalency courses, and trained inmates in interpersonal skills and job-retention skills. We offered transcendental meditation, provided individual counseling, and developed a rigorous physical-development program. We believed that the only way to get out of jail was to grow your way out—not blow your way out. We used the principles of training as treatment, based on Carkhuff's groundbreaking work in the 1960s. Instead of chasing old demons and traumatic experiences into fruitless sinkholes of the past, we got the inmates to focus on the present and taught them how to respond to pressured situations in the moment, but only in constructive ways.

Our best training ground was on the basketball court. Individually, we were out-skilled at each position, but we never lost a game. In the gym, the inmates' life themes revealed themselves: These individuals didn't work as a team because they didn't know how to use each other's strengths. They got tired and quit. They got mad and quit. They took stupid shots that had little probability of going in. They made poor choices for shot selection. They were only interested in showy offense, not gritty defense. Sound familiar?

On the other hand, the jail rehab staff consisted of a bunch of slow men and women (yes, half the staff were women) who together had a fair number of skills: We knew how to work together as a team. We knew how to get the ball to the right person with the right shot. We leveraged each others strengths. We hustled all the time. We never gave up. We played tough defense and made wise shot selections on offense. We communicated with each other and supported each other to hold down inmates who had exceptional individual ability.

We learned more about the inmates' lives in one hour on the basketball court than we could have learned in 10 hours of counseling. It was physical. It was their world. It was real. There was no hiding behind words and excuses. We used the insights from the basketball court as content for our counseling.

"Hey, Freddie, remember that hook shot you took from the corner the other day? What were your chances of scoring with that shot? How do you think that relates to the way you live your life? Do you think you are making any investment in time and energy at something that has a reasonable chance of success?"

These same principles apply to creating an organizational soul: Training programs have to be real. The content has to connect directly to employees' everyday lives. Hard questions need to be raised that get each person's attention.

The jail rehab program was clearly a success in quantitative terms, but more importantly, the program succeeded in qualitative terms. Inmates in our program experienced moments in their lives that they had never experienced before. We listened. We cared. We believed they could learn and change. Over time, *they* came to believe it, too. That's what happens when there is an organizational soul.

As I write this book, America now has more people in jail than any other country. In fact, while we account for less than 1% of the world's population, we house 25% of the world's inmates. More than 30 years after we published the results of our program at the Kalamazoo County Jail, states are finally starting to invest in inmate rehabilitation programs.

My search for corporate soul continued when I landed in a hospital. I was asked to head up a corporate-health promotion program for Samaritan Health Service, a multi-hospital corporation in Phoenix, Arizona and one of the largest employers in the state.

Samaritan was one of the first hospitals to enter the wellness business. It seemed a little odd that a corporation that made its money on sick people would go into the business of keeping people healthy. In this case, it was a decision based more on image than soul. The hospital wanted to position itself as a premier provider of comprehensive health services. It wanted to offer services along the full health continuum. Even so, the fact that Samaritan would pursue a broader vision and offer health-promotion programs to its own employees reflected a hint of an organizational soul. We called our program "LifeWise," and offered a wide range of programs that were designed to free people from the consequences of unhealthy habits.

We even used FREEDOM as an acronym to describe the components of our effort. It stood for:

- Fitness
- Risk Reduction
- Educated Eating
- Emotional Well-Being
- Drug Decision
- Occupational Health
- Management of Stress

We hired an extraordinarily talented team of 15 health professionals, including psychologists, physicians, nurses, fitness instructors, nutritionists, and educational specialists. Since we were one of the first comprehensive, hospital-based wellness programs, I was asked to deliver keynote speeches at national conferences all over the country. I was also asked to chair a consortium of multi-hospital systems representing over 500 hospitals nationwide to explore the possibilities of including wellness in their range of services. I mention these things because the combination of PR value and the real contribution of wellness to the stated mission of the hospital might lead you to assume that other health care institutions would rapidly embrace this innovative service. Not so. The dearth of response gave me my first insight into the myopia and lack of soul in most organizations.

My work with Samaritan Health Service helped me land in the closest thing to corporate heaven you'll ever find. In 1982, AT&T hired me as a consultant to help them manage changes associated with their impending divestiture. AT&T, before the break-up, was a unique animal in corporate America. At that time, it employed over a million employees and had a monopoly position in the telecommunications industry. Since AT&T was a regulated business, it determined annual budgets by creating dream lists of new services and then raising rates sufficiently to cover its budgets and achieve a reasonable return on investments.

AT&T's mission was universal service, and I can say without a hint of redness in my face that employees believed in the mission and acted accordingly. It was a service-minded company that treated its employees with dignity and respect. It may have been maternal (there were good reasons it was known as Ma Bell), but it was respectful. Thus, it was not a leap at all for AT&T to decide to create a comprehensive, culture-based wellness program for all its employees. At the time, AT&T was one of the first companies—along with J&J and Control Data—to embark on this new way of supporting healthy lifestyle behaviors among its employees. Building a vital, energetic, healthy workforce did not run counter to its

DNA. AT&T believed in serving its employees, just as it believed in providing great service to its customers.

With the full support of the executive committee, we designed, developed, and delivered the Total Life Concept program—the first of its kind in corporate America. And we evaluated its impact. In fact, we had a team of 14 Ph.D.s, including outside evaluators, who measured the differential results between control sites and intervention sites. We found that the Total Life Concept not only reduced projected health care costs by $300 million over a ten year period, but also that the program increased morale, satisfaction, and productivity. These results were published in the *Journal of the American Medical Association.*

The health, economic, and productivity results of comprehensive wellness programs should push corporations to rapidly embrace this kind of innovative approach. Again, the dearth of corporate response to AT&T's innovative program gave me my second insight into the myopia and lack of soul in most corporations.

What made the AT&T program unique was its focus on the culture. We offered the full range of health promotion programs (fitness, nutrition, weight control, smoking cessation, stress management, wise medical consumerism, change management, healthy relationships, etc.), but we concentrated our efforts on the corporate culture. We extended the notion of risk factors to include the norms and values of the workplace.

I ended up dedicating most of my professional work to creating healthy, innovative and productive work environments. In America, during the time I was growing up, people's health became progressively worse. Obesity rates went sky high. Activity levels reached all time lows. Americans ate fatty food and too much of it. Restaurants believed they needed to serve portion sizes three times the size of what was required in order to satisfy customers. We super-sized everything, and we became super-sized as a result. Staying healthy in that culture was like swimming upstream. All the support was heading in the wrong direction. That's what creating organizational soul is all about: changing the current. It's easier to swim downstream than it is to swim upstream, and you are less worn out at the end of the day.

I tried to get the attention of senior leaders to create healthier work environments. I wrote a book called *The Complete Guide to Wellness*. It sold very few copies. I wrote books on Spiritual Leadership, Ethical Leadership, Leadership Myths and Realities, the Leadership Lexicon—they too sold very few copies. It was becoming crystal clear that my search for organizational soul was like trying to find a needle in a haystack.

In 1990, I founded and chaired Summex, the first integrated health-management services company in the country. We worked with many large organizations, including Sears and NYNEX, to integrate benefits, fitness, clinical services, disability management, organizational development, and training with the goals of increasing organizational productivity, reducing health-care costs, and improving quality of life. In every demonstration project we took on, we achieved all three goals. Summex was recently sold to WebMD for $40 million, even though the comprehensive solutions we offered were never broadly embraced.

I decided that the solution called for a frontal assault on corporate culture. The formula for corporate culture change is fairly simple:

> Leaders must serve as role models for desired values, norms, and behaviors. The rewards and recognition systems need to be aligned with those values, norms, and behaviors.

It was a strange path to this point: war, jails, hospitals, schools, corporations. Each venue gave me a different perspective. And each pointed to the same conclusion: We need to develop a *soul* if we are ever going to dig ourselves out of the deep holes we have dug for ourselves.

Part 2:
The Principles

Imagination is the eye of the soul.

— Joseph Joubert, *Pensées*

— 2 —
Why Would an Organization Want or Need to Create a Soul?

If every interaction, day after day, is viewed as an opportunity to create a meaningful work environment, the possibilities for organizational soul will eventually take root. Those roots will provide the foundation for growth.

If an organization only focuses on taking what it can get out of people at any cost, the organization won't have the slightest chance of creating a soul, independent of any words to the contrary. When words and actions are congruent, people are more motivated.

If an organization focuses only on getting its fair share, then, at least, members of the community can do their work with a sense of satisfaction. When people feel good about what they are doing, productivity improves.

If an organization focuses on giving each stakeholder opportunities to grow, members of the community will want to come to work. When people are aligned with a larger purpose, passion develops.

If an organization focuses on helping everyone with whom it interacts, then the organizational soul will evolve. When customers experience an organization's commitment to help, partnerships emerge and trust builds.

If an organization strives diligently to discover new possibilities against the backdrop of its reality, then it may establish the conditions in which substance and soul will take root.

When people are continually thinking about what's possible, innovation increases.

If the organization creates a soul, then all of its stakeholders will live to grow. So why create organizational soul? Because you will...

- Increase motivation
- Improve productivity
- Heighten passion
- Strengthen partnerships
- Deepen trust
- Increase innovation
- Experience faster growth

Motivation, productivity, passion, partnerships, trust, innovation, and growth are the ingredients you *must* have if you are to get extraordinary and sustainable results.

Part 3:
The Possibilities

Soul. The word rebounded to me, and I wondered, as I often had, what it was exactly. People talked about it all the time, but did anybody actually know? Sometimes I'd pictured it like a pilot light burning inside a person. Or a squashy substance, like a piece of clay or dental mold, which collected the sum of a person's experiences—a million indentations of happiness, desperation, fear, all the small piercings of beauty we've ever known.

— Sue Monk Kidd, *The Mermaid Chair*

— 3 —

Creating Soul in Business

How would you recognize an organizational soul if you saw one? After searching for 20 years, I finally found a corporate soul at Lotus Development Corporation in Cambridge, Massachusetts. Lotus was the developer of the initial spreadsheet tool 1-2-3 for the personal computer. It sold a million copies the first day it was on the market, and launched Lotus as a high tech powerhouse. By 1990, Lotus had sales of $1B and 4,000 employees. Its headquarters was built alongside the Charles River in Cambridge.

Jim Manzi, a McKinsey consultant to Lotus who was later hired to head up marketing for the company, eventually became president and CEO. Manzi hired Russ Campanello as his VP of Human Resources, a bright, thoughtful, talented professional with high decency and high integrity. One of Russ's first assignments was to define the company's operating principles, which would guide behavior and inform decision making. The executive committee at Lotus took these operating principles seriously, and implemented policies and programs to support them.

As a visible way to support work-life balance, Lotus created a program to encourage healthy lifestyle behaviors. It was called Healthy Partnership because the employees and the corporation would work together to create a healthy and productive work environment, and would share the benefits of the partnership. There was a fair attribution of responsibility and a fair distribution of savings from the program. The Healthy Partnership Program used a gain-sharing mechanism that gave points to employees for healthy behaviors and making wise health-care consumer decisions. Lotus had projected health-care costs to increase at 15% per year for the next few years, so it agreed to share any savings with employees who participated in the program if health-care costs rose less than 15%. Thus, if health-care costs were predicted to rise $2 million dollars in a given year but they only increased $1 million during the year, Lotus would distribute $500,000 differentially among participating employees. It used the remaining $500K to pay for the investment it made in the Healthy Partnership program. This is a great example of corporate soul, because it tangibly communicates that we are in this together—we are *true partners in health.* Employees were encouraged to take time for themselves to stay fit, manage stress, get preventive health checks, and attend to their families. At the same time, Lotus expected its employees to be responsible, productive, and innovative.

Lotus encouraged its managers to engage in meaningful and respectful conversations with employees. It mandated training for all managers, and required participation in a management fundamentals course as well as an advanced management course. These programs taught managers what they needed to know to comply with the law and internal policies, but they also instructed managers in how to give constructive feedback, develop employee capabilities, and inculcate desired norms and behaviors. The programs focused on four key principles of leadership:

1. Know and grow yourself.
2. Know and grow others.
3. Know and grow the business.
4. Know and grow your customers.

Managers were taught how to assess performance and potential, as well as how to identify the blind spots of their employees. The training emphasized the importance of leveraging strengths and following through on commitments.

To make sure that creating organizational soul at Lotus was more than just words and empty promises, its executive committee set up a "Soul Committee" whose sole purpose was to identify the gaps between stated values and day-to-day behaviors. This committee consisted of representatives from all levels of the organization and all departments. The Soul Committee met once per month to discuss cultural strengths and concerns, and it presented a summary of its discussions to the executive committee once per quarter.

In essence, Jim Manzi had the courage to appoint a "court jester" to point out incongruities between words and actions. What gave the Soul Committee real credibility, however, was that the executive committee was willing to take action on its recommendations. Because it was inclusive and visible, the Soul Committee had broad impact on the culture. Leaders were expected to model desired behaviors, and people were rewarded for behaving in ways consistent with a soulful culture.

Soul Work

Over the past few decades, I have worked with many organizational leaders who understood the connection between organizational soul and productivity. To demonstrate the broad range of outcomes possible when you create organizational soul, I invited several of them to write about their experiences creating soul within their respective organizations. While none of these efforts was officially labeled "soul work," they all had the common elements of soul development: meaningful work, employee engagement, deep dialogue, and continuous reflection and improvement. If the idea of creating organizational soul seems a little "soft and fuzzy" to you, their experiences might change your perception. They demonstrate that creating organizational soul has been the most important factor in achieving results across a variety of organizations. And the results are not only dramatic, they are also significantly different from the results that come out of organizations without soul.

Maintaining an Organizational Soul
in a Fast-Growing Company

Jesse Haines, head of Marketing for Google TV Ads;
Google Radio Ads; and Google Print Ads

When I meet a new person for the first time, I try to get that initial gut sense of who he or she is, based on energy level, eye contact, and facial expression. When I walk into a company for the first time, I can instantly get a "vibe" that provides the first view into the organization's soul. When I entered Google for the first time to have my third of what would be a total of eight interviews (the first two had been over the phone), I immediately caught a whiff of a culture that was distinct from any that I'd experienced before.

I saw, with my own eyes, many of the things I'd read about in the countless articles about Google and its culture. As I waited in the lobby for my host, I watched young hipsters in jeans flying through the halls on scooters. Through the glass doors, I could see people in conference rooms sitting on fat, brightly colored exercise balls as they intensely discussed issues during a video conference. And as we walked to the interview room, we passed brightly lit micro-kitchens stocked with countless types of organic juices and bowls of fruit, and lined with plastic bins full of nuts, cereal, crackers, and cookies—an indication of just one of Google's most famous employee perks: free food.

More interesting than the cool accoutrements, however, was the energy that filled the air at Google. There was a palpable sense that **things were happening**. The people in the hall wore expressions of thoughtfulness and intensity,

(continued)

rather than the typical corporate haggardness that pervades the cube farms of many of the companies I'd worked with during my days as a management consultant. And when I sat down to chat, face-to-face, with the "Googlers" tasked with interviewing me, I was impressed by their curiosity in the *whole* me. They asked tough questions, not only about what I might bring to the table as a marketer for Google, but also about what made a good teacher (I had taught high school history way back when) and how I would redesign the interface of Froogle to drive more clothing sales (I had previously come from an apparel retailer). My key take-away from that day: the gourmet food and fun toys are only physical manifestations of the Google soul. **The soul itself is animated by the people at Google, and is manifested through their work spirit.** The organizational soul and individual soul feed each other.

But how, in a company that hires lots of people every day and is opening offices all over world, is it possible to foster and maintain the Google spirit?

My vantage point on Google is from the business side. I was fortunate enough to make it through the Google interview gauntlet. Now, two years later, I run marketing for what Google refers to as our "traditional media businesses": Google TV Ads, Google Print Ads, and Google Audio Ads. These are small start-ups that are betting on Google technology to deliver more accountability, relevancy, and measurability to the 30-second spots, newspaper ads, newspaper ads, and radio jingles that advertisers and

(continued)

agencies are buying to reach their target audiences. How have we built the organizational soul on these teams?

First and foremost, we created soul by focusing on the people. Take Google TV Ads, for example. As this operation was getting started, we needed to find people who knew the TV ad-buying business—this was unfamiliar territory for Google, and some native guides were critical. But as we started interviewing, we saw that even those who checked out on all the right levels of experience did not make the final cut, unless they possessed that undefinable, I-know-it-when-I-see-it, entrepreneurial, curious Googley factor. We were willing to wait for the people who were the perfect fit. And it's the reason why all Google candidates (myself included) have to go through so many interviews with so many different people in the organization.

We also put the word out within Google to see who might be interested in going on a bit of an adventure. One interested party was a talented young woman from an unlikely neck of the woods, the finance department. She wanted to do sales, and in spite of some initial reservations, she gave us enough reason to think that she could. Equally important was the fact that she was a Googler who'd been around for a while and could help instill the Google soul in our fledgling group. A year later, she's one of our top account executives, as well as a bedrock of our team.

Secondly, these start-up traditional media businesses have benefited from Google's unwritten principle of "Ask forgiveness, not permission." The spirit of this is not, of

(continued)

course, to encourage Googlers to intentionally break rules or fly in the face of authority, but to encourage our people to take good ideas and run with them. Fast. Google has always kept its organization flat. Titles don't mean much at Google—they are simple, and describe what we do: engineer, marketing manager, vice president (though we have very few of those). Long, fancy monikers like Senior Executive Vice President are non-existent. We don't care much about titles, because we believe that good ideas come from everywhere. After all, our founders were two grad students who came up with a great idea in the dorm. And when someone has a good idea, Google wants you to make it happen quickly. It's the reason why our engineers have 20% time to work on a project of their choosing; it's the reason why there are people whose job it is to ensure that there is **not** a lot of red tape bogging things down.

After TV Ads was launched and business started to roll in, we noticed that our account managers' time was being consumed by the arduous task of creating charts to summarize the interesting second-by-second tuning data for their clients. "Could we outsource some of this work?" suggested a 26-year-old account manager. With a few nods of encouragement from the team, he set about figuring it out. A few weeks later, he presented a nifty online form where team members could check off the data they required and send it to two Google associates in our India office who would package it up into a nice and tidy chart. A few phone calls, a bit of planning, and a lot of get-up-and-go was all it took. The initiative is in action today, and

(continued)

now the account management team spends their time strategizing with clients, rather than wrestling with charts. In this instance, a strong organizational soul bred efficient organizational operations.

And finally, since I know you're wondering about it, let's get back to the free food, discount massages, the Authors at Google lecture series, and the game room complete with Guitar Hero and a Wii station. Are these great perks just recruiting tools, or are they related to the company's organizational soul? I would argue it is the latter. At the heart of Google's organizational soul is a commitment to following your passion. Larry Page and Sergey Brin followed their passion to organize the world's information and make it universally accessible and useful—and created Google as a result. The people who work here often choose to come to Google because they are following their passion—for technology, for ideas, for innovation, for making the world a better place. As we all know, when you are passionate about what you're doing, you are likely to excel. And that's where all the perks come in. If you are immersed in a project, it makes it a lot easier to stay in that headspace if you can just walk down the hall and grab a healthy lunch. It is often times when people are relaxing—taking a run, in the shower, or getting a massage at Google—when we have those game-changing ideas. If someone has read a great book or heard a great new song, Google wants him or her to celebrate that with the community. Our lectures are all employee initiated—we invite authors, singers, artists, politicians, and chefs to come to

(continued)

Google so that passions can be shared and we can keep the air rich with that energy that makes us all know that **things are happening.**

On the traditional media team, as on most teams at Google, we encourage people to take advantage of all that Google has to offer. When I run into my team members at a celebrity chef cooking demo or an author's lecture, the thought running through my head is not *Why aren't they at their desk working?* And they aren't thinking *Oh crap! The boss caught me goofing off!* On the contrary: We're thrilled to have discovered that we share a passion and can talk about ways that we might incorporate an idea or technique from the lecture into some of the projects we're working on.

At Google, we work hard to find the right people, give them license to pursue their good ideas, and create an environment that makes it easy to celebrate and revel in one's passions. It worked for Google's Search business, but can it work for some of these newer ventures? No one can be sure, but this past quarter our TV, radio, and print businesses hit an exciting revenue milestone that we weren't expecting this early on. Things are looking good.

Creating Organizational Soul
in a Large Company

Mike Forney, former CEO at AT&T

It was 1982, sixteen years into my career as a public relations specialist for AT&T. The corporate chapter of my working life had been both exciting and rewarding. The compensation was good. Promotions had occurred with some regularity, and the career challenges were demanding but exhilarating.

It was at this point that I first became aware that institutions large and small had unique cultures and principles, often unspoken but deeply ingrained, that permeated the way things were done. The AT&T culture became evident to me when the company was faced with an anti-trust challenge that would eventually destroy it.

I thrived in the underlying culture at AT&T. It was consistent, if not strongly maternal and self-satisfying. Business decisions were logical. Management treated employees fairly, and in my personal experience, it concerned itself with individual careers, growth, and individual opportunity.

That changed as the specter of a federal court-dictated divesture loomed. The needs of those we referred to as "the general body of rate-payers"—the families, shopkeepers, and businesses that relied on POTS (plain old telephone service)—ceased to be an operating priority. The "new" customers were high-end businesses and other customers who demanded state-of-the-art communications, new technology, and marketing glitz. (It wasn't until later that AT&T's senior management learned how savagely

(continued)

competitive this market was, a reality for which they were woefully unprepared.)

Seemingly overnight, traditional AT&T managers were replaced with marketing "whiz-kids" whose only credentials were résumés from high-tech companies and fledgling enterprises. Even before the final divestiture hammer fell in 1984, AT&T had been transformed into a polyglot of people, messages, and values that never, in this writer's view, coalesced into a recognizable corporate "soul."

After playing a leadership role in the communication of the "new" AT&T to customers, employees, and investors, I ended my 18-year career there to pursue more-satisfying work. Although I did not fully comprehend it at the time, the move provided an opportunity for me to create an organizational soul, albeit one dramatically different than AT&T's.

I joined two consummate salesmen to form a regional commercial mortgage banking company in 1985, created initially as a spin-off from a highly respected residential mortgage company. We three partners built the structure, acquired new companies, and expanded the business over the next 14 years, before selling it to a national company in 2000.

The values we had created for our business drove every decision during those years, and carried over in the sale when we insisted that the business and our employees would continue to function with the same ethical standards and commitments to our customers and our employees.

(continued)

Ironically, those values and operating methods were so evident that barely three months after the sale, during the transition phase between the two companies, I was asked to assume the duties of chief operating officer of the parent company.

The major challenges we faced included the need to instill the culture of our smaller, entrepreneurial business into this larger national company and position it for expansion and eventual sale. This was accomplished over the next two years, and culminated in the sale of the parent company for $46 million.

Understanding one's values and implementing them in the day-to-day operations of a business is challenging, to say the least. At AT&T, it was more a matter of momentum. Because the he corporation was so large, it was inexorably slow to change course and was nearly impossible to stop.

Coalescing around a set of values is a challenging process, compounded by the number of those who agree to share those values. In our small company, it began with three partners, the assistance of outside counsel, and the use of a few standard personal evaluation tools (e.g., Myers-Briggs). That was the easy part.

Who among us would quarrel with the notion that integrity, service to customers, and loyalty to colleagues are appropriate business values? The real effort is in the doing, rather than the saying. More importantly, how meaningful would these values be if they weren't shared by every employee and demonstrated in every transaction, every day?

(continued)

Creating a business culture or "soul" requires a strong foundation. The process includes developing organizational values, gaining commitment, testing the values in the real business world, revisiting them regularly, and living up to them when violating them "just a little" would be far easier.

We used several comprehensive surveying techniques to identify commonly held values of the partners, senior managers, and staff. What did each of us think was important? How did we rate ourselves and our company in these areas? How did each group respond to the question surrounding the overarching theme *"How do things work around here?"*

It should not have come as a surprise to find wide gaps among the groups of partners, senior managers, and staff about key values both in words and in practice. Although initially troubling and frustrating, these disparities opened the door for honest and non-threatening discussion that helped eliminate inconsistent policies and behaviors. We developed an organizational soul that enabled us to deal openly, honestly, and directly with hard issues—and get results.

Creating Organizational Soul
in a Small Business

Julie Meek, founder and CEO Emeritus of The Haelan Group

Creating organizational soul is the key ingredient for the success of any organization. With soul, an organization has the best chance of thriving, growing, and sustaining its core purpose. Without it, an organization struggles, starts and stops, wastes millions of dollars in lost profits and productivity, and simply creates a miserable experience for all involved, including employees, their families, managers, executives, board members, and shareholders. To me, organizational soul is the single most important prerequisite to success, and creating it intentionally has to be the primary foundational work against which all other business decisions are filtered. It's the solid and ever-expanding trunk of the tree—many branches will eventually sprout and then sub-branches and leaves will form, but all of this growth is dependent upon the healthy trunk. When the trunk isn't healthy, a branch may survive for awhile, but eventually the tree falls. You even see branches with green leaves on a fallen tree, but they don't survive long.

In 1995, I founded a health management business, The Haelan Group, to solve one of the most pressing problems we are facing today: the unrelenting surge of health-care costs. But we were among the first to apply empirically-validated social and behavioral science to the solution. It was our vision to find (and help early) that ten percent of an employer's population that was about ready to become seventy-to-eighty percent of the current year's health-

(continued)

related claims and lost-productivity costs. We developed a very unique predictive modeling tool that has become the industry standard for finding this group of people prospectively. We also developed the health coaching model that helps this high-risk group determine how they wish to improve their health and accomplish their goals for improved levels of feeling and functioning.

Doesn't all that sound logical? As a CEO facing double-digit increases in your health care costs, wouldn't you run to purchase this service? We thought so, but we found out that our ideas were perceived by prospective clients as revolutionary and impossible to accomplish. What resulted was a hard ten years of proving our worth to the industry and moving from a few early adopters to a robust and long-term set of happy clients.

As you might imagine, this kind of business is all about recruiting and enlisting the passion of great, talented, and highly professional people. This business requires the best of the "helping professions," working as a cadre of service-minded people to take care of customers: call center workers, survey scanners, account managers, sales and marketing folks, and most importantly, our coaches. In essence, the entire operation is focused on creating the best interaction between a high-risk person and his or her coach and/or a person with a question and our call center. It is an intensive, highly interpersonal and highly tailored service where we want each person receiving our services to feel as if the entire company is there to serve them—at their

(continued)

time of need, and in a way that is totally unique to the set of factors causing them to feel "ill."

As the company's founder and CEO, as well as the scientist behind our predictive modeling and coaching methodology, what I was absolutely sure of was that we would not succeed without organizational soul. So we made a conscious decision to create the most robust organizational culture we possibly could to support and align our people with our collective vision.

So how did we do that? The answer isn't simple or finite. It was an ever-flowing series of decisions and efforts by not only me, but also our leadership team and our employees. All were responsible and all participated, which made our culture enduring and strong. I was awed through the fourteen years that I led the organization at how many times I could have made a decision that would have destroyed all the "soul" we had built together. I was awed by how strong yet fragile "soul" really is. All the good can be destroyed by a decision that is out of alignment with the soul of the organization. All the stakeholders are watchful, always assessing how the many decisions and behaviors and words of each day match up against our "soul."

But to be pragmatic for a moment, we had some guiding principles that we lived by that went a long way toward guiding our thoughts, words, and deeds day-by-day:

- People came first—those we served, our clients, our employees, and our vendor partners.

(continued)

- When there was conflict, we sought more information. We tried to understand, not to judge. We came together, not looking for ways to sabotage or get ahead or derail another person.

- We expected results and were very clear about expectations.

- When mistakes were made, we viewed the situation as an opportunity to learn, not to punish.

- We celebrated great results and great efforts with lots of fun. We were rich with praise.

- We cared for each other when we were hurting, and went out of our way to acknowledge and cover for each other when personal situations demanded priority and attention.

- We adhered to a common set of values, and even when it was hard, we lived our values, often at our own expense, in order to do the right thing.

- We tried to help our industry get better by participating actively in our professional organization and speaking out about changes that were important.

- We rarely hired people who turned out not to fit our culture, but when we recognized a hiring mistake, we quickly and humanely helped people leave.

One of the best things we did was to create a very transparent performance and compensation reward system.

(continued)

Creating Soul in Business

Every employee, no matter what level, led their own quarterly dialogue session with their supervisor. The discussion template included:

- My dream or mission in life
- How I spend my time; whether my "job pie" is changing; and whether the changes are appropriate or need attention
- My accomplishments this quarter, including how I did on agreed-upon bonus goals
- My struggles, whether professional or personal, and what kind of help I need to break down barriers to great performance
- My beginning ideas for goals for next quarter
- My feedback to my supervisor, and in general, how I feel about the company

All employees had a 10% quarterly bonus opportunity tied to an individual and team goal agreed-upon with their supervisor. As CEO, at the beginning of each quarter, I led the leadership team to develop the company's priorities and their own goals. The leadership team then subsequently encouraged goals among their direct reports that aligned with the company's overall targeted goals for the quarter and the year. Imagine this: Even when we had only 20 employees, we accomplished 20 x 2 goals each quarter x 4 quarters per year = 160 results a year that would not have been accomplished had it not been for this amazing system.

(continued)

Each employee had direct and clear feedback on how their salary was set according to compensation surveys we paid for biannually, and feedback regarding where they stood on their salary level, compared to the median for their job. So people were very clear about how to make more money, and they thrived on accomplishing what it took to get there.

The second most important attribute of our company was a very open, transparent communication style. We communicated it all: the good, the bad, and the ugly. So, even when times were tough, people hung in there because they knew I wasn't hiding anything from them. If I couldn't share, I explained why, but gave them enough of an idea. They knew the challenge, what I was doing about it, and how likely we were to solve the problem at hand. Rather than alarm people, this style gave people a sense that they didn't have to waste any time wondering or "filling in the blanks."

So what were the fruits? First and foremost, soul creates incredible employee loyalty. Through the worst of times, we had virtually no turnover. People came to work dependably. It was rare to have someone call in sick. We had laughter and fun and craziness in the office. We had smiles. We had very low health-care costs. We had people begging to work for our company, and literally had the pleasure of 10:1 ratios of applicants-to-hires, regardless of the position we were hiring for. We earned the respect of the industry for our integrity. We won awards for "Spirit"

(continued)

and "Innovation" and "Entrepreneurial Growth." In short, we grew the company's family from a handful of people interested in our vision to over 500 people invested in just over a decade. We reached about 2,000 people in the beginning, and have now swelled to over a million people coached over our history. That's something to jump out of bed for! Our results—improvements in health and financial outcomes for our clients—are the best in the industry, and grow deeper and better with each passing year as we continue to funnel our learning into our products and services.

In short, we found that developing "organizational soul" was the glue that held us together and helped us overcome all the obstacles to our collective success. Developing "soul" requires collective intent to value it, to filter decisions against the impact on it, and to intentionally grow it. The rewards for those who choose this path make it all worth it!

Creating Organizational Soul in Corporate America through Health Promotion

Molly McCauley

Is it hard to imagine that organizational soul exists in corporate America today? I suspect that based on what you hear and read, you would reply yes. Corporate executives being charged with and convicted of insider trading, CEO salaries exponentially surpassing those of the employee population, and cost manipulation to maintain a favorable Wall Street image are fodder for your opinion.

But let's move beyond the headlines and consider a brief journey into the day-to-day workings of corporate America. Imagine entering the headquarters lobby of xyz company and being greeted by a receptionist—perhaps even needing to make your way through corporate security. What now? Where would you go, who would you talk to, and what would you see to suggest that the company has organizational soul? Perhaps there are indicators.

- A visit with the CEO reveals details about a newly formulated strategy to assure shared decision-making.

- The Human Resources director summarizes a vision to integrate parts of the organization to focus on Health and Productivity Management.

- The senior manager of Training and Development highlights available courses, designed not only to develop *workers* to do their jobs, but also the *individual* to build his or her personal skills base as a family member, a social being, a community contributor, etc.

(continued)

- Observe employees, working as a group, who are smiling, laughing, and seemingly pleased in the moment.

- You see an interaction between a manager and an employee that is obviously respectful and collaborative.

In summary, the examples listed above paint a picture of an organization comprised of numerous individuals with soul who commit every day to make the organization better. In turn, their efforts build and coalesce, and eventually become organizational soul.

That is where I come in. For the past 30 years I have dedicated my career to molding a piece of the organizational maze and making it the best it could be, not only for those who planned and implemented the services (the staff), but also for those who participated and realized the health benefits (employees and their families). In my work as director of Health Promotion for a very large corporation and a much smaller corporation, I worked with talented health promotion teams to:

- Create an environment that supports positive behaviors.

- Influence management to sponsor and advance health programs that significantly impact the health and productivity of employees.

- Function as a cohesive staff dedicated to a common vision and mission.

- Celebrate the plethora of stories from individuals whose lives were improved by the programmatic emphasis on positive health behaviors.

(continued)

- Contribute to the corporate bottom line through reduced health-care costs and increased productivity—in turn, contributing to corporate viability and shareholder value.

More pragmatically, on a day-to-day basis, how does it happen? Much like the "soul" committees that play a key role, I believe there are "soul success factors" for worksite health promotion that also play a key role. Those success factors ensure that the right things happen for the right reasons. However, I would be the first to admit that while there are times when everything works well, there are also times when things don't go smoothly. The **soul success factors,** detailed below, highlight my experiences from two different corporate environments. When it works well, a little more soul is breathed into the organization, and when it doesn't, you will begin to pick up on things that are characteristic of soulless organizations.

Staffing and Organizational Support

Programs don't just happen. Planning, development, and implementation of any program resides with the staff. Just how well that staff delivers depends on how they work as a team, how they interface across the organization, how they are supported by all levels of management, and how they know they are getting results.

Teamwork. Building a staff that develops a genuine respect for the talent and contribution of each member is

(continued)

no easy task. However, individuals who have the opportunity to meet frequently, build trust in the talent of others, and communicate openly are likely to focus on the mission and goals of the program. Performance feedback is very important. A well-designed performance-management program affords the staff member feedback from managers, peers, and internal customers and fosters positive growth. One significant negative is when there are team members who work against the leaders of the program. Undermining decisions becomes the norm for those individuals, and often the team is splintered. Addressing the problem openly and quickly is a must.

Cross-Organizational Relationships. A health promotion program that does not work across the organization is doomed. If the program does not build the ties necessary to become mainstream within the corporation, the program staff will spend most of the time doing "their" work, and will still be considered "them." The goal is to make it *us*. You can find numerous ways to communicate if you tap into Public Relations. You can make health visible in the environment if you get the support of Facilities Management (building services). You can make healthy eating a reality if you form a partnership with Food Services. You can enrich the safety-related components of the program if you work with Environmental Health and Safety. And you can integrate the work of prevention by working closely with Benefits and the health plans. The goal is to get as many employees to succeed in meeting their personal

(continued)

goals as possible. It simply cannot be done alone. Seek out the influencers and make them your champions, no matter where they work in the organization. They are your "value-added"!

Management Support. I've heard it said for years—management support is critical to the long-term success of the program. Yet I have watched programs thrive with just the annual allocation of a new budget, and I have watched programs fail with line managers who have been fully engaged for years. Face it—support is fleeting. It hinges on financial issues, the business environment, and the multitude of organizational priorities, domestic and international. Personally, I think the best manifestation of management support is when line managers engage with their employees, discuss health goals for the group members, and support each other in the accomplishment of those goals. The line managers encourage the use of the fitness center, arrange departmental coverage so that screenings can be attended, and remind employees about attending the Health Fair. Beware of a senior executive who blocks your access to the CEO and the key decision makers. Beware of the managers who tell you they don't need hard data because they can decide based solely on intuition. Beware of the manager who insists on a strategy that is not a fit with the wants and needs of the population. Under such circumstances, you will spend a lot of time swimming upstream.

(continued)

Getting Results. Nothing is more gratifying or more motivating than knowing that what you are doing is impacting key measures: Health risk levels are decreasing and health status is being improved. Employees are satisfied with the focus and strategies of the program. There is a documented decrease in health care costs and disability costs among those employees who are actively using the program. The corporation enjoys the successes of the program and in turn recognizes the value proposition: employees are healthier; productivity is greater as energy and "presence" increase; and health-care costs are positively impacted. At the end of the day, these gains improve shareholder value.

The Program

Laying the foundation for a program that is just getting started, implementing the program using the best principles, and leveraging ongoing changes to make the program better are all part of the life-cycle of any program.

Getting Started. Make sure that the program is designed to meet the needs of the entire population. Recognize that each and every individual is important, and be sure to have something in the program that appeals to each person. Recognize that employees and their families have different health issues, and that each one should have the tools and resources to improve or maintain their level of health. Include primary prevention, so that those who don't have

(continued)

the disease don't develop it. Include secondary prevention so that everyone understands how to recognize and address signs and symptoms of illness and injury. And include tertiary prevention, so that those who have chronic conditions can learn to manage their condition and avoid complications. If the focus of the program is too narrow or skewed to a specific group, an "us/them" mentality sets in and has a negative impact on the program.

Implementing. Honor the diversity of the population by selecting methods and strategies that appeal to different styles and cultures. Everyone learns differently. That is why it is so important to offer print *and* electronic materials—brochures, email, videos, webcasts, self-paced learning modules, etc. Hold large and small events, conduct screenings, make health counseling available, and set up an information table to disseminate key information. The main thing is to appeal to the entire population in one way or another.

Change. Change is a good thing. It is true that not all changes represent progress, but remember that there is no progress without change. Changes to the health promotion program help renew interest, demonstrate a commitment to new strategies, and reflect a willingness to learn from programs in other organizations that are achieving quality results. I have seen programs derail under their own weight when they are not nimble enough to change. It is

(continued)

easy to maintain the status quo; it takes courage to change for the good of the participants.

Making a Difference

Nothing can be more rewarding than knowing you are making a difference in the individual lives of the employees and their families. If you motivate by using incentives, you will achieve strong participation and you will make a difference. If you teach the principles of health behavior so individual health changes are successful, you will make a difference. If you are proactive and emphasize personal choice without being prescriptive, you will make a difference. When you personally care about what you do and find joy in doing it, you will make a difference. Look broadly at the message within this book, and celebrate your role in Creating Organizational Soul.

– 4 –

Creating Soul in Social Service Agencies

I have had some of my most fruitful searches for soul in the most unlikely places. Perhaps the most soulful team on which I ever worked was at the county jail described in Chapter 1. My colleagues and I cared for each other, we supported each other, we had each other's backs, and we were passionate about our work. We formed strong bonds. We built a healthy, innovative, and productive work environment. We set high standards and expected each member of the team to carry his or her weight. While we put more demands on the inmates than they had ever experienced in their lives, we still treated them with dignity and respect.

I have found that people who work in social service agencies have a helping orientation. The nature of the work attracts people who want to make a difference in the world. As a rule, there tends to be less competition, greed, and pretentiousness in social service organizations. There is usually a strong sense of community and shared purpose. Values are not only clear, they come alive every day.

In my work with social service agencies, I facilitate the annual strategic planning meetings in which we re-visit the vision and mission to see if they need "tweaking." We review progress on goals and objectives, and we discuss how we are exhibiting the core values of the organization. At the beginning of each meeting, I ask the board and staff members to share stories that illustrate how the core values are "alive" in the organization. I'm always struck by how easily and enthusiastically people are able to share stories that make the words real. These stories always include moving tributes to colleagues and volunteers who have gone beyond the call of duty to demonstrate caring, respect, trust, and service excellence.

The stories I selected for this section were written by the CEOs of three amazing organizations with whom I have worked over the past 25 years. Dr. Betsy Hall has transformed Homeless Solutions in Morristown, New Jersey from a small shelter for homeless persons to a comprehensive service that offers transitional housing, affordable housing, and a range of supportive services. Bob Lomauro has transformed the YMCA in Somerset Hills, New Jersey from a ramshackle fitness facility with a handful of dissatisfied members and annual operating deficits to a 12-million-dollar state-of-the-art wellness center with 20,000 highly committed members. Evelyn Savage has transformed the Visiting Nurses Association of Somerset Hills, New Jersey from a small home-health-care organization to a world-class social service agency that provides a full range of services, including adult day care, hospice, and clinical care.

In all three cases, the agencies were not only able to grow their facilities and budgets, but they were also able to instill a sense of spirit and joy in the communities they built together. Yes, they improved the quality and quantity of their services, but they also provided enriching experiences for their boards, employees, volunteers, and clients. In these stories, they will share how organizational soul contributed to these transformations.

Creating Organizational Soul in
a Not-for-Profit Organization

Dr. Betsey Hall, CEO of Homeless Solutions Inc.,
Morristown, New Jersey

I think of soul as the heart of the organization—those ways of being that make an organization alive and passionate about the work. I think of the energy, imagination, and creativity that one brings to work and the desire to make the many tasks of the work add up to the climax of success and achievement. Somehow soul, life breath, and life-force work together. The justice orientation of our goals is that of making life and lives better, creating systems that are responsible and responsive, inviting all players to think, act, and lead for the good of all.

How do we create soul at Homeless Solutions? I think it is by being drawn into the notion of acting justly, doing justice, and being fair to others and ourselves. I suspect it has to do with wanting the best for people around us, including the clients, tenants, and the (homeless) guests on whose behalf we work. Also, we demonstrate respect and care for our donors. Without their support, help, and energy, we could not be the vehicle for bringing help.

I imagine it has to do with treating others as we want to be treated. Always looking for ways to stop and reach out to each other in genuine care. I love the recent story of the young woman who was playing softball for her college when she hit her first homerun. On her way to first base she pulled a muscle, and could not go on. Rules prohibited her teammates from helping her around the bases, so the

(continued)

other team helped her get the winning run by carrying her around the bases! Now *that* is passion and compassion, leadership, and action! Imagine an organization with that kind of soul. Imagine a world with such abundant compassion.

Why is it so important?

Without soul, you have only individualistic, competitive self-promotion. It is important for the soul of an individual to create a living and working space that has soul—a place that reaches out beyond itself. An organization with soul goes a long way past goals and strategic plans and the present moment, reaching the touchstone of the importance of all life. The sweet place where we all want to be valued and respected, accepted and appreciated, loved and remembered.

How did we create it?

We have tried over the last year to make an effort to show our appreciation for all that our staff does for our guests. We have been very good at showing our donors how much we appreciate them. More could always be done for both.

I think organizational soul is created by my not hogging the stage or the praise and by recognizing the good work we all do. I do not need ego strokes for my work. I have a strong enough sense of myself and my strengths. I know my weaknesses and ask my staff to fill in where I need help. I let them know that I can't do it all, because I do not

(continued)

have all the skills (and I need them) and because I will not burn myself out doing their jobs. I want *them* to succeed and get better, and I want *them* to get credit and be recognized in the community. I want everyone who is in the organization to be a community representative for HSI. I want people to grow into their full selves. I work with people to encourage them—not to discourage them. I want everyone, me too, to go home at night feeling good and wanting to stretch to the next level of development.

I recently asked my director-level staff, "If you were my boss, what would you like me to be doing?" What great responses I got! What thoughtful and helpful conversations we had. Things I did know and things I could not have known. Everyone appreciated the time to talk individually about something larger than their specific work—to have an opportunity to think about the big Homeless Solutions picture. To hear some of my thinking on where we are going and to have some input into those thoughts.

I am not sure how to create organizational soul, but I think it comes from the leader. And I think it has to do with respect for others and an earnest desire to learn and listen and be honest and truthful. I used to say about leading a church: "A church is only as healthy as its lead pastor." I think that is true of any organization and any government.

(continued)

What results did I see?

HSI is a healthy, successful, and growing organization. I see an organizational desire and ability to think big thoughts and to move in that direction. I see a staff willing to work hard, but not needing to prove they are working hard by staying late and coming in early! I encourage all staff to take all their vacation and time off. I have just asked the leadership staff to make space in their month for a day of creative learning. I don't care what that is. I want them to read, relax, travel, and to see what others are doing. I want them to stop and let their imaginations carry them to a new place. I hope to see them grow in ways they want to grow. And I expect we will grow as a result.

The soul-growth in individuals reflects on and in the work of helping guests grow, donors opening their hearts, and the organization reaching its goals. I think we are seeing people growing and not being crushed by their work.

Our products, services, and solutions are better as a result. Guests put their lives back on track and we help other organizations. Members of the community feel good about having helped others and each other.

Creating Organizational Soul in the YMCA

Bob Lomauro, CEO of the Somerset Hills YMCA

Twenty-five years ago, the Somerset Hills, New Jersey YMCA was operating in a run-down building, had a small and declining membership, and was on the brink of bankruptcy. Today, its 85,000 sq. ft. state-of-the-art facility has three swimming pools, a large wellness center, a gymnasium, a teen center, a state-licensed child care center, and various multi-purpose and social gathering spaces. It is the center of community life in Somerset Hills. Its annual operating budget has grown from $500,000 to $12 million, with a membership in excess of 20,000 children and adults of all ages. It took a lot of soul searching to get us from where we were to where we are today.

During this past year, the Somerset Hills YMCA has continued its journey of self-discovery—defining who we are and where we are, but more importantly, what we would like to become.

There is a strong desire among our staff to find a shared vision, an "organizational soul," if you will, that we all can embrace, individually and collectively. We hope that this vision or soul will become the vehicle that will drive and direct us toward the achievement of our association's mission: helping people to achieve their God-given potential in spirit, mind, and body.

What is *organizational soul?*

I believe organizational soul consists of an over-arching culture that truly defines its beliefs and attitudes and

(continued)

enables the organization to achieve competitive advantage, while developing its staff and serving the community. It is the essence of our being.

Our YMCA's culture is no different today than what it was when the first YMCAs were founded some 150 years ago. We are about teaching and demonstrating the character values of caring, honesty, respect, and responsibility. We are about helping people to meet the universal needs of having meaning and purpose in their lives. We're about helping people to feel a sense of belonging. We're about developing friendships. And we're about accepting people.

The Challenge

Our YMCA, like many others around the country, has adopted the four core values of character: caring, honesty, respect, and responsibility. We have incorporated these values into our marketing and printed materials and have worked hard to systematically infuse them into all of our programs. We proudly hang colorful banners throughout our facility indicating our endorsement of these high ideals.

However, the real challenge for our YMCA is to make certain that our teaching and demonstration of these core values are not empty words. When we put the values out there as what we stand for, we are going to be judged based on those standards. If we do not consistently use the four values as our blueprint, we are sending a mixed message about our commitment to character. Every staff

(continued)

member is a role model, and each is responsible for strengthening our YMCA's culture.

How do we create organizational soul?

So, what do we need to do to truly walk the talk of character development?

One of the first things is to establish a strong link between character development and staff development. There has to be support for people in the organization who stand up for what they believe. A culture shift will only take place when there are rewards for the right behavior. By systematically hiring people of good character, by incorporating values education in all staff training, and by establishing "character" success measures, we will have our best shot at building and sustaining a "character culture" at the Somerset Hills YMCA. We will have done what we can to create organizational soul.

Creating Organizational Soul in the Visiting Nurses Association

Evelyn K. Savage, CEO of the VNA in Somerset Hills

Organizational soul is the life force of an organization. It is organic and must grow from within the organization. It cannot be imposed from the outside. Creating organizational soul is purposeful, not accidental. Leading an organization with soul infers working with people with diverse talent to overcome the limitations of the organization and of individuals so that individuals and the organization can soar beyond real or perceived limitations.

In my earlier work life, I was in a middle-management position in a visiting-nurse agency that served people in Newark, New Jersey and 11 surrounding communities. We were organized into teams, and confronted very daunting social and health-care challenges every day. However, it struck me that the incredible stress that was pervasive throughout the organization was internal workplace stress. The stress we all dealt with in our patient and family interactions was not debilitating like the stress caused by an administration that had great difficulty asking the difficult questions, such as: Why are good clinicians leaving employment after an average of two years? Why are messages so negative, and rarely positive, regarding how someone is performing? Why aren't problem-solving strategies employed in a more systematic way? Why do the walls of the office seem to exude stress?

The soul of this organization was sick.

(continued)

Efforts to create change in this environment were met with resistance, and I lacked the power, which only created further frustration and stress. I vowed that if I had the opportunity, I would create a workplace that is fair and just that encourages and rewards excellence, and that promotes professional and personal growth.

That opportunity came when I took the position of executive director at the Visiting Nurse Association of Somerset Hills in 1984. Nearly my entire career has been in the community health, non-profit sector. Specific challenges faced by leadership in that arena are a need to work with a volunteer board; often limited financial resources; dependence on a variety of highly regulated fee sources; and a scarcity of experienced professionals and paraprofessionals. Furthermore, the sector has become very competitive.

In 1984, our VNA was a small, well-regarded 80-year-old organization that employed 20 staff, had a board of more than 30 individuals, served a population base of 50,000, and had a budget of less than $1M. It provided home health services, had just initiated a hospice program, and provided public health and school nursing services in the communities it served. It had a well-established biannual fundraiser, and was supported by two local United Ways. There was a history of support for staff education, paid for out of a special fund named for two prior long-term directors who were champions of education.

(continued)

From that small beginning 25 years ago, this VNA has grown to have a diverse staff of 135, and more than 700 volunteers serving two counties in central New Jersey, with a budget of over $7M and a state-of-the-art facility that is mortgage-free. Recent patient satisfaction results place this agency in the top 5% of home-health-care organizations nationally. A recent staff satisfaction survey showed an overall satisfaction rating of 70%, 7 points higher than the national benchmark. We have been fortunate to continue to attract board members with diverse talents who are willing to provide the governance and support necessary to continue the mission of the VNA.

Why is organizational soul important?

As adults, we spend a significant percentage of our life at work. The quality of this time impacts on each individual's feelings of self-worth and well being. In an organization that provides a critical service to people, those delivering that service are more likely to perform in an optimal and caring manner toward patients if they are satisfied with their job, have a sense that the organization respects them and is concerned about them as individuals, are treated fairly, and have opportunities for growth.

As a member of the Governor's Commission on the Shortage of Nurses in 1988-1989, I listened to testimony from so many nurses whose major concern and frustration was that they came to the end of their day and felt that they had not been able to care for their patients sufficiently

(continued)

well, because of excessive workloads, lack of equipment, and/or support in their workplace. Nurses wanted fair compensation, but their overriding concern was their ability to provide excellent care for their patients.

The shortage of nurses eased after a number of changes, including improved wages. However, 20 years later we have a pervasive and long-term shortage of nurses once again. Sustainability of change, not temporary fixes, was what was needed, but it was not achieved on a widespread basis.

The impact of *soul* in an organization has financial implications also. When we do an excellent job in delivering home health care, hospice care, community health programs, and adult day care services, our work is appreciated by the community. This appreciation is expressed in a willingness to volunteer time and invest money, via charitable contributions, in the organization. In turn, these resources bolster the organization's ability to continually improve elements of the workplace and the excellence of service delivered.

How did you develop organizational soul?

The staff and the board needed healing after several years of turmoil, and the staff in particular were very wary of a new leader. I came well prepared educationally, with experience at a staff level, as a middle manager, in upper management, and as a consultant. However, I had not been in the executive director seat before. I considered the two

(continued)

years spent as a consultant to home health agencies, fledgling hospices, and public health agencies throughout northern New Jersey as a critical management training experience! It provided an up-front-and-personal look at what worked and did not work, both programmatically and in terms of leadership style.

My leadership style is one of consensus building, with an eye on the goal of excellence. I believe in leading change, not reacting to it. I also believe in working collaboratively with other organizations and individuals; and in seeking to influence the broader health-care arena through leadership positions on the board, in committees, or in other health-care organizations.

Policy changes, service area expansion, and program enhancement needed to be conceptualized, communicated, and operationalized in a way that got both board and staff buy-in. Given the growing complexity of the business, increasing competition, and limited financial resources, my problem solving/decision making process has to always take into account congruence with mission and fairness to employees. This has required knowledge of the business environment, willingness to take risks, and a strong network of colleagues in the home-care/hospice/public health/geriatric arena.

I have a strong belief that each individual needs to be the right fit for a particular job. I have been fortunate that my leadership style and commitment to excellence in patient care are congruent with the VNA history and board leadership. Over the years, the organization has attracted

(continued)

staff that are skilled and caring professionals. An organization is not successful and does not have soul because of one person, but rather as the end result of a strong team who are committed to a common purpose and who exhibit mutual respect for one another and for those they serve.

Education has long been highly valued and supported by the VNA, and thus there was a strong foundation on which to build. Opportunities and financial support to seek undergraduate or graduate degrees were expanded from the nursing staff to the entire staff in 1991. More recently, there has been specific encouragement for staff to seek certification in areas of clinical specialty.

There has been a recognition that as the population ages, a broad array of services are necessary to assist individuals to remain in the community, to keep people optimally functional, and to support caregivers as they strive to balance care of a loved one with other work and family obligations. Over the years, we have established an adult daycare center, expanded a program of respite support to caregivers, established caregiver support and caregiver education, partnered with other community agencies to provide low-cost emergency alert devices, and carried out a number of other supportive-care initiatives.

What results did you see?

We began with a staff of 20, a small budget, a limited geographic area, and a facility that was built for the organization in 1906. We now serve a large geographic area in a

(continued)

new facility with an annual budget of $7 million. More importantly, we are providing better service to more people with a broader reach.

State-of-the-art training facilities, a clinical skills lab that is unique in a home-care/hospice setting, and an expanded adult daycare facility with personal care amenities, a staff that embodies excellence, mutual respect, and an embrace of change—these have helped us develop a strong and growing organizational soul.

There is no doubt in my mind that we could not have achieved the results documented above without deliberate attempts to create an organizational soul.

—5—

Creating Soul in Education

My wife taught special education for 28 years. She worked with Down Syndrome kids, neurologically impaired kids, learning-disabled kids, and emotionally disturbed kids. I have never seen anyone bring so much care and compassion to the classroom as she did. It wasn't easy. She worked hard. Teaching is not a 9 to 5, nine-month job with lots of vacations. She typically arrived at school at 6:30 in the morning, and brought work home at night. It was not unusual for her to spend several weeks in the summer getting ready for class. She brought imagination and creativity to her work every day. She demanded a great deal from her students, but they never doubted her love. She retired in 2008, still fresh and full of love. I can't think of a better example of bringing soul to an educational institution.

Early in my career, I worked at Amberly Elementary School in Portage, Michigan as a consultant. My job was to help the teachers improve their interpersonal skills, content development skills, and teaching-delivery skills. One of my favorite memories of those two years was when I conducted a competition in the school to see which student in each grade could identify the most "feeling" words to describe their experience. To establish a baseline, I simply said, "Please write down as many 'feeling words' as you can think of." Not one student was able to identify more than ten—feelings were not something they talked about. And they certainly couldn't identify and express the feelings they were feeling.

I worked with all 22 classrooms over the next few weeks by discussing the different categories of feeling (e.g., feeling "down" or feeling anger, fear, or confusion) and the different levels of intensity (high, medium, or low). For example, a high-intensity "up" word might be *thrilled,* and a low-intensity "fear" word might be *concern.*

After two weeks, I asked the students again to write down as many feeling words as they could. Some students wrote down as many as 400 words, including wonderfully descriptive words like "dancy" or "fancy." Over a two-year period, the whole teaching community (for the most part) tried to encourage students not only to identify how they were feeling and how their classmates were feeling, but also to talk about the choices they had on how they acted on those feelings. Together, we created a learning community that validated feelings and encouraged kids to make healthy choices. Over time, we expanded on the interpersonal training and empowered the kids by teaching them problem solving and planning skills.

Several years after we created this constructive environment, Amberly was granted a national award for excellence in education. I believe that the soulful environment we created in the school contributed to that award.

In this section, I have asked two people who are close to me to describe their experience in creating organizational soul.

The first contribution to this section is by Bill O'Brien, a long-time business colleague of mine who as done terrific work creating organizational soul in a variety of settings. The second perspective comes from my oldest daughter, Rebecca, who was inspired by her mother to enter the teaching profession. Rebecca earned a master's in Education and taught for five years in the Bronx. She is now a fourth-grade teacher in Brooklyn and has just completed work for a second masters degree (this time in Literacy), at Columbia University.

Creating Organizational Soul at a University

William O'Brien, Board of Trustees for Life University

In 2004, Life University, once the largest chiropractic institution in the world, was about to lose its accreditation from both the CCE (Council on Chiropractic Education) and the SAC (Southern Accreditation of Colleges). Students, some as much as three-quarters of the way through the program, were packing their bags and driving to other colleges, pleading to be accepted in order to complete their studies. The Life campus, located just outside of Atlanta, became a ghost town. Life was dead.

Life University was once the brand name in chiropractic training for integrity-based health and wellness education. In 2004, it was deeply in debt and about to close. The college's president, the highest paid college president in the country (yes, more than Harvard, Stanford, and Yale), had been dismissed. The board of trustees had two prevailing concerns: The first was to renew accreditation and get students back to campus. Second, and more importantly, the board had to account for what had happened and prevent it from happening again. Here are the steps we took.

1. We took an honest accounting and assumed complete responsibility for the disconnect between the culture we wanted and the culture we created.

   Although the board had plenty to be upset about regarding the administration, we needed to assume responsibility for what occurred. We needed to personalize our role. We had allowed our core values (integrity

(continued)

rigor, student-centeredness) to be compromised by a seductive set of alternative values, such as money, celebrity, and profit margins. We allowed aggressive marketing and its results—more students—to feed our collective image of ourselves as the best and the brightest in the business. What we hadn't anticipated was our lack of ability to service this large number of students on a small campus with a small budget. Being the largest college in the profession superseded discussions about how to give each student the time, education, and resources to acquire the knowledge and skills needed to become a great chiropractor.

2. We started a soul-searching process.

   We began an introspective process. We decided that it was not enough to tell the CCE and SAC accreditors that we had a plan to reorganize and get back into compliance regarding education standards. We decided that it would be better to close the school than to allow students to graduate without experiencing the true vision, value, and purpose of alternative-based wellness care with the degree of rigor, passion, and educational standards that we had always wanted. The board hired a new president based almost solely on his love of the chiropractic profession, his passion for the profession's future, and his ability to articulate and inspire others toward the vision, values, and purpose of wellness-based health care.

(continued)

3. We identified and articulated the culture and organization we wanted.

As a board, we spent a year battling the day-to-day crises of getting back our accreditation, our financing, and our students. Simultaneously, we entered a year-long process, as a board, to determine exactly what we wanted and needed to be, who we wanted to graduate, and how we could achieve this. We created a document that every student, faculty member, parent, alumnus, and prospective student was required to read. The document outlined eight core principles that we wanted to represent the total experience at Life University (e.g. integrity, respect, scientific inquiry, and ethical leadership).

4. We took accountability for the gap.

The board then formalized a process for assessing, developing, implementing, and monitoring all Life University programs for the inclusion of these core principles. Today, all students must take a one-week course, given by the president, in the development and integration of these eight core principles in student life. An academic master plan was created and is being implemented and continuously improved each year. The board, which now consists of many new members, operates in standing committees, short-term task forces, and virtual teams. Each member is required to participate actively in the board's get-well plan.

(continued)

5. We created generative, strategic, and fiduciary plans.

The board's process now involves continuous discussions that include generative (possibilities) questions, strategic plans, and fiduciary updates. The administration works closely with the faculty and alumni to exchange ideas that help to improve the campus.

Life University received its full accreditation once again in 2006. A review of the campus in 2008 resulted in exemplary marks from both CCE and SAC. Life students today rank number one in post-graduate testing on state and national board exams. The campus is thriving, and measured, qualitative student growth continues.

Through a values-based introspective process, we were able to shed the illusion of celebrity and status and to tell the truth about who we are and who we want to become. We grew a soul. We got our "Life" back.

Creating Soul in the Classroom

Rebecca Bellingham,
Berkeley-Carroll Elementary School, Brooklyn, New York

When you enter a classroom with soul, children will look happy and engaged. They will greet you with a handshake and a smile, and they will look you in the eye. They realize they are ambassadors for the room, and they feel proud to show you around and introduce you to the learning and traditions that occur every day inside their room. A classroom with soul is a powerful place of intellectual and emotional growth. Every child feels certain he has a place, that he is important, and that his job is valuable.

A classroom with soul doesn't occur by accident, however. It happens through the daily activities, rituals, and traditions that a teacher builds into the children's day. In my classroom, and many others in my school, I use an approach called "The Responsive Classroom" to build community, independence, and accountability into my room. The Responsive Classroom was started over 25 years ago by educators who believed in bringing together social and academic learning throughout the school day.

Every morning, students in my room are greeted with a message that compliments their hard work from earlier in the week and forecasts upcoming events, activities, and projects. "Good Morning Powerful Readers" the message might read, or "Hello Mighty Mathematicians!" or "Good Morning Cooperative Classmates." Every morning, they remember how powerful, smart, thoughtful, and eager they are. They are reminded that their hard work, focus, and

(continued)

cooperation is valued and expected. At the end of every message, there is a space for them to solve a problem, write a thought, or share the title of a book they are reading or piece of writing they are publishing. From the moment they arrive, they know they belong. They enter a classroom that welcomes them and makes space for them to ask questions, raise ideas, and share work.

Every morning, we also start with a quick meeting to greet each other, do an academic or social activity, and share news from our lives and about the day. We practice how important it is to look each other in the eye, listen to each person's words, and use a positive tone of voice. Children know their actions and tone matter, and they realize the importance of showing care and concern for each member of the classroom. In fact, when a classmate is absent, we sing a song entitled, "Nothing is the same without (the name of the missing student)!" Even when children are not present, we remind them that they are essential to the wholeness of our community and classroom.

In a classroom with soul, there is an energy, an eagerness, and a sense of excitement about the daily activities and work to accomplish. In my classroom, students work cooperatively and individually to complete tasks that are meaningful and relevant. They are not asked to write a story about a topic I have chosen. They learn to be real writers and write stories that *they* have generated from powerful moments in their lives. As a class, we learn strategies to write stories that are rich, well crafted, and meaningful. I teach a whole-class mini-lesson abut writing

(continued)

or reading, but I coach students in different ways, depending on what they need and what they are gesturing toward doing well as readers, writers, and thinkers. In my classroom, I try my best to meet the individual needs of every student, knowing that all kids don't need the same thing. That is an overwhelming task, of course, but it forces me to know my students and find ways to grow each of them differently. In this way, I hope students realize that I know them well, and that I see them, understand them, and understand how to best teach them.

In my classroom, you hear the words, "Help your friends out" quite a bit throughout the day. When we are transitioning to a new activity or getting ready to go to a special class or recess, or when I have used a signal for all-class quiet, you will hear me say, "Help your friends out." In this way, I am reminding students that they can help each other remember how to get in line efficiently, stop talking, or prepare for the next activity. Students remember they are part of a community, a place where individuals work together to achieve a desired result, instead of a place where certain kids get praised repeatedly while others are perpetually chastised. I hope that my students become the kind of people who are mindful of each other and who think cooperatively and collectively, instead of the kind of people who are simply out for themselves.

At the end of every day, we meet again for a very brief closing circle. We might share a word that describes our day, something we are thankful for, something powerful we learned, a way someone helped us out that day, or

(continued)

something we are looking forward to accomplishing that week. Once again, we come together as a community, even for a brief moment, to share our experiences, our hopes, and our thanks.

In a soulful classroom, children leave school feeling accomplished and appreciated. They leave school knowing that their work and their words have been recognized. And, I believe, they come to school each morning looking forward to the day ahead.

It takes work to create a soulful classroom, but the results are worth the effort. Kids are happier, more engaged, more responsible, and more compassionate with one another.

Summary

The stories in this chapter illustrate the possibilities that are realized when an organization embarks on the journey to develop its soul. The personal experiences of these corporate and non-profit leaders will help you recognize a soulful organization when you see one.

You know an organization has soul when you hear people saying...

- We trust each other.
- We feel empowered.
- We engage in meaningful dialogue.
- There is a high level of reflection on critical issues.
- We engage in healthy conflict.
- We are passionate about a higher purpose.
- There is a high level of creative energy.
- We are inclusive.
- We are always learning.
- We are caring and compassionate.
- There is a high level of integrity.
- We value and respect differences.
- We are genuine.
- We are brutally honest about the facts of our situation.
- We encourage growth and well-being.
- We seek ways to help each other succeed; we collaborate.
- We are committed to the organization.
- We hold each other accountable.
- We drive for results.
- We are open, honest, and direct.

(**Note:** You will find a tool for measuring soul in your organization in Appendix 1.)

Part 4:
The Pain

You need chaos in your soul to give birth to a dancing star.

— Friedrich Nietzsche

— 6 —
What does a soulless organization look like?

In the last chapter, you learned how to recognize an organization that had soul. It's not that hard. It's even easier to recognize a soulless organization. As my daughter wisely observed in a particularly soulless organization, "There's no dancing in these halls." Here are the 10 basic indicators of a soulless organization:

Indicator #1: People look tired. After a series of suicides and workplace homicides, a major auto manufacturer asked me to design and implement a stress-management program. My first response to the client was this: "Implementing a stress management program in this environment will be like putting a band-aid on cancer. What you really need is a comprehensive people-and-culture initiative." When I learned that the company was inviting its top 500 executives to a conference in Orlando, I managed to get myself invited so I could observe the executive team. What I saw was stunning. Most executives were significantly overweight and under-energized. Instead of walking with a bounce in their step, eyes wide open, chin up, erect, and vital, they shuffled from one meeting to another with their chins down, eyes drooped, and back and shoulders slumped. They looked pale, exhausted, and worn down—the walking wounded.

When I reported these observations to the study sponsors, they agreed with my assessment and asked, "When can you start with that stress-management program?" I replied, "All of the state-of-the-art stress programs available aren't going to change this problem. You need to change the soul-sucking norms that are draining the life out of the people who work here." Within a few weeks, funding for the "stress" program was cut and our work was ended. There is still no dancing in those halls.

Indicator #2: High turnover. After several key people suddenly left this same organization, I was asked to conduct an analysis of the root causes for the unusually high turnover. Management had assumed that the key issues revolved around workload and work-life balance. This organization had been asked to take on more and more work, but headcount was frozen. That meant that the remaining staff had to suck it up and work harder. The fact that turnover had spiked only exacerbated the problem. What I found as a result of the interviews and focus groups was that while workload and work-life balance were clearly a problem, they paled in comparison to other factors that were present: lack of trust/respect, micro-management, poor communication, and lack of clarity. People weren't complaining about working long hours—they objected to being hovered over, harassed, left in the dark, and not being clearly informed about their roles, responsibilities, and decision rights. Yes, they were getting burned out, but workload was a minor part of the problem. The reason people weren't excited about coming to work in the morning was because of what the leadership was doing (or not doing) and the things that were being rewarded in the culture. There was no dancing in those halls.

Indicator #3: Conversations are disingenuous. We are all influenced in some way by the constant pandering and "spinning" we hear on nightly news programs. It's hard to discern these days what is truth and what is manufactured to suit a particular purpose. In this culture, people tend to create their own version of the truth, independent of reality and without the inquiry required to get to the real deal or root causes of an issue. In my work at large bureaucratic organizations, I see many executives who pretend that they know what they are doing or that everything is "on track," when it is obvious to anyone paying attention that the work is a train wreck waiting to happen.

Many organizations are in the middle of large transformational efforts, whether it's HR, IT, R&D, or whatever. It is not uncommon in such situations for people to pretend that they are making progress, when in truth they are simply spinning their wheels and wasting time. The unwritten rule is not to expose the reality. Employees notice immediately that there is a big gap between what is being presented and what is actually happening. When leaders move up the leadership ladder into positions of increasing responsibility and visibility, they have a vested interest in appearing to have a substantive command of their role, when in reality, they can only deal at surface levels. In short, they can't peel more than one layer of the proverbial onion, but they pretend they run deep. There is lots of dancing in those halls, but it's only around the issues.

Indicator #4: If there is a mistake, the solution is to cover it up. In a soulless organization, the norm is to cover up mistakes and inappropriate behavior. People don't take responsibility for their part of the problem. In governmental organizations, we are seeing a lot of sexual misconduct and abuse of power that undermine any attempts to create soul. Whether it's an inappropriate liaison on the part of a governor, corrupt practices by a mayor, inappropriate behavior on the part of a U.S. president, or prisoner abuse by members of the military, the effect is the same. People ask, "Where is the soul of this organization?" Cover-ups only aggravate the problem and increase the cynicism toward leadership. Conducting and hiding underhanded dealings create mistrust, cynicism, divisiveness, and alienation—all the elements that kill soul. If a chemist wanted to create a soul-killing compound, these would be the right ingredients. Fortunately, living in an electronic environment makes such cover-ups more difficult to get away with.

Indicator #5: There is a short-term focus. The tyranny of short-term focus is that quarterly results are always king and investments in long-term strategies are discouraged. The culture is driven by numbers. People are seen as dispensable, so employees don't feel valued. Stress rises dramatically the last month of each quarter as employees are pushed to bring in the numbers, even if it means pressuring customers and cutting bad deals.

Indicator #6: The organization doesn't learn. The cultural immune system spits out any person or idea that doesn't conform to existing patterns and norms. There is no effort to seek out different ideas, ethnic groups, or relationships. When mistakes are made, people are not gathered together to reflect upon what went wrong and what to avoid the next time. When projects are completed, debriefing sessions are not held to identify what worked, what didn't work, and what was learned.

Indicator #7: Training and development efforts focus on weaknesses. Discussions revolve around how to eliminate weaknesses, instead of how to leverage strengths. At best, people are put into training programs to shore-up a deficiency instead of being given assignments to refine solid competencies and stretch and challenge them. At worst, performance management is seen as a way to weed out the poorest-performing 10% every year.

The Center for Creative Leadership, a non-profit organization committed to developing leaders worldwide, reports that 70% of an employee's growth comes from job assignments, 20% from coaching and feedback, and 10% from training. Further, the return on those investments is significantly greater when the development opportunity focuses on leveraging strengths instead of eliminating weaknesses. Unfortunately, most of the training budget goes to correcting weaknesses—the area with the least chance for return or satisfaction. This is a soul-diminishing experience.

Indicator #8: Managers act unilaterally. In organizations without soul, employees are not involved. There is a lack of involvement in decisions that affect them. Leaders believe that sending an e-mail *after* a decision is made is sufficient. People do not believe they have a voice in how things work. Managers dictate what happens, instead of engaging in a dance in which all opinions are heard.

Indicator #9: The organization violates the environment. There is very little thought given to the size or impact of the organization's carbon footprint. Leaders dance around regulations and stomp irresponsibly on the earth, instead of treading lightly and carefully on it.

Indicator #10: Critics get the most attention. The organization suffers from squeaky-wheel syndrome, where managers try to chase down sources of dissatisfaction, instead of focusing on providing meaningful jobs and recognizing people who are satisfied and thriving. Leaders dance with the whiners, instead of freeing exemplars to create their own dance.

Summary

The 10 indicators described in this chapter are based on my experience with soulless organizations. You could surely list your own. Essentially, however, it comes down to this: There is no joy in a soulless organization. There is no sense of connection, community, collaboration, or caring. There's no dancing in the halls of a soulless organization. (**Note:** See Appendix 2 for a measurement tool.)

Part 5:
The Poisons

— 7 —

What are soul derailers, and what causes organizational train wrecks?

In his last book, *The Coldest Winter,* David Halberstam writes eloquently about the price soldiers had to pay in the Korean war because of the arrogance and lack of inquiry of its regional commander, General Douglas McArthur. McArthur refused to listen to intelligence reports on the gathering strength of the Chinese Army along Korea's northern border, and ordered his troops into what turned out to be a needless blood bath. He exhibited two of the traits of the most dangerous leaders: He was extremely decisive, and he was extremely inaccurate.

This section describes seven "poisons" that soulless leaders inflict on an organization. The effect of these leadership poisons can't begin to compare to the pain of American soldiers who died in the frigid fields of Korea, but together, they suck the soul out of any organization, and diminish the outcomes. The list begins with the two poisons exhibited by McArthur and detailed by Halberstam: arrogance, and lack of inquiry.

Poison #1: Arrogance. The first and deadliest poison is *arrogance.* The arrogant leader's "walk down the hall" is more often a strut than a stride. The nose is pointed more toward the ceiling than the floor. Eyebrows are raised a bit below the frown on the forehead. When you are in a meeting with an arrogant leader, you don't usually get to complete a sentence, because they cut you off to interject their "profound" point of view. Arrogant leaders are typically very decisive, independent of their depth of understanding. They are firmly convinced that their perceptions equal the truth, even though reality tells a very different story. When *you* do something right, this kind of leader takes credit; when something goes wrong, you get blamed. Their ego fills the room as soon as they enter—in fact, their whole persona reeks of vanity. The antidote to arrogance is humility—a choice arrogant leaders typically reject.

Poison #2: Lack of Inquiry. The second poison for a soulful culture is *lack of inquiry.* Non-inquiring leaders are convinced that their instincts are always correct, and resent people who question their authority. They seek to be understood, not to understand. If you ask too many questions, you can expect to be punished. These leaders rarely invite people to challenge assumptions and to raise differing points of view. Court jesters and messengers are killed. There is typically a rush to judgment, because these "leaders" don't like to dig for facts. There is no evidence of evidence-based decision making. Reflection and rigor are not valued. The antidote to lack of inquiry is healthy curiosity—a cure these leaders can't tolerate.

Poison #3: Exclusivity. The third poison is *exclusivity.* It's all about the club. These kinds of leaders surround themselves with clones and sycophants. They love executive dining rooms, luxury cars, corporate jets, reserved parking, and private clubs. They want to make sure that the thickness of their carpet, the size of their offices, and their window views are at least equal to anyone else's. They only select from Ivy League schools and are seduced by pedigree. Involvement is not a word that resonates with them. Loyalty is valued above competence. They prefer to make unilateral decisions (and then inform people after the fact). The antidote to this poison is inclusivity—a cure that runs counter to all their inclinations.

Poison #4: Greed. The fourth poison is *greed.* The mantra for the greedy leader is "More is better." These people are looking for personal aggrandizement. They are not known for crediting others, celebrating team successes, or making a contribution. They see information as power, and use it to increase their personal advantage and agenda. They drip with envy for those who have acquired the trappings and toys that wealth brings. These leaders are more focused on taking and getting than they are on giving. They are seen by their peers as competitive and independent, instead of collaborative and interdependent. They are seen by their customers as pushing products and services, instead of building solutions and partnerships. Their names do not appear on anyone's list of trusted advisors. The antidote to greed is charitable giving—the very thought of which makes greedy leaders gag.

Poison #5: Condescension. The fifth poison is *condescension.* While it is a close cousin of arrogance and exclusivity, condescension manifests itself in particularly ugly ways. Condescending leaders tend to be mean-spirited and selfish. They have no appreciation for the power of kindness, support, and recognition. They abuse their own power instead of looking for ways to recognize and learn from others' power. They would much prefer to look down than look up. You know you have encountered a condescending leader when you finish a conversation feeling belittled and wounded. Condescending leaders make you feel less rather than more. People who work for condescending leaders do not feel appreciated or valued. The antidote to condescension is concession—a pill these leaders find hard to swallow.

Poison #6: Close-mindedness. The sixth poison is *being close-minded.* Close-minded leaders lack self-awareness and are not open to feedback or help from others. This poison has close "chemical" ties to lack of inquiry and to condescension, but it is even more deadly because it kills innovation, new ideas, visions of possibility, risk-taking, and passion. It sucks the soul out of the organization. Close-minded leaders are focused on why ideas won't work, instead of how they might work. They tend to be defensive, resistant, and rigid. They're famous for saying, "We've tried that before," "That won't work here," "Color me skeptical," and "No way!" You know when you are working for a close-minded leader when you don't see much creativity, spontaneity, or excitement in the organization. The antidote for closed-mindedness is openness—an injection their minds are closed to.

Poison #7: Controlling. The seventh poison is *controlling for purposes of power* (micromanaging), instead of "freeing" for purposes of empowerment. Controlling leaders hover and harass instead of delegate and support. They reward conformity instead of creativity. These leaders are most easily recognized by how different they are from leaders who value initiative.

Contrary to micro-managers, freeing leaders encourage leadership at every level. People are encouraged to assess their levels of leadership in all domains of their life: relationships with significant others, relationships at work, and relationships with community. When you ask to be given time off to contribute to a community event, controlling leaders say no. Freeing leaders say yes. When you tell a controlling manager you have signed up for a personal development course at night, she or he will tell you not to let it interfere with work. A freeing leader, on the other hand, will congratulate you and ask you to look for ways to apply your learning in all areas of your life. A controlling leader will expect you to be an observer or participant at work. A freeing leader will expect you to contribute and lead in every aspect of your life. A controlling leader will want to make you one-dimensional. A freeing leader will encourage you to be multi-dimensional and will be concerned about your wholeness and wellness. A simple chart like this can help you assess what your leader expects from you in every dimension of your life.

	Personal	Significant others	Work	Community
Leader				
Contributor				
Participant				
Observer				
Detractor				

Great leaders encourage and empower people at all levels of the organization to move up the scale in every aspect of their life. In the personal domain, people are encouraged to develop physically, emotionally, intellectually, and spiritually. In dealing with significant others, people are supported in their efforts to develop meaningful relationships with the people they care about. At work, people are encouraged to innovate, initiate, and integrate. In the community, people are encouraged to get involved in civic organizations and make contributions to the areas in which they live, learn, and work.

It's easy to recognize the effect of controlling leaders. First, many people will be functioning at the detractor level: they are out of shape, out of touch, and out of sync with their own values. Many others will be functioning at the observer level: they are simply watching life go by. They are better critics than actors. With less-controlling leaders, you will see more people at the participant level: They will be engaged and fully involved in a multitude of activities that build their personal lives, their relationships, their work lives, and their community. With freeing leaders, you will see most people at the contributor level: they are continually looking for ways to add value to significant others, to colleagues, or to community services. With truly soulful leaders, you will see most people functioning at the leader level: they step up to make things happen, and they have an impact wherever they go, independent of title or rank.

When formal leaders operate at the detractor level in any dimension of their life, they are going to have a poisonous effect on others. If they are workaholics who pay no attention to significant others or community services, their behaviors and actions will send signals that balance and wholeness are not valued. If they don't read and don't continually inquire about the world in which they live, they will become one-dimensional automatons who don't exactly inspire development and growth.

Leadership is not defined by title. It's defined by impact. Every person in an organization should evaluate where they stand in these four dimensions of life. These ratings should be private and confidential, but each person should be encouraged in public forums to assess how they are doing, and to commit to moving up the scales. In that kind of environment, wholeness, uniqueness, and development are valued.

Summary

Even great companies have soul killers. In established companies with well-institutionalized core values, a few leaders can not only tarnish the image, but also undermine the substance of the culture. The problem with weaving values into the fabric of the organization is that people take them seriously and notice when they are frayed.

Conversely, soulless companies usually have good people who take heroic actions to make the work environment a better place to be. These leaders can be found in work teams where there is a high level of passion and enthusiasm for the work and a high level of support for each other. These pockets of soul can serve as an antidote to a toxic work environment. These teams simply stay focused on what they need to do and do what they can to help each other succeed.

This section described the poisonous leadership behaviors that derail careers and kill organizational soul. It also identified the key antidotes: humility, curiosity, inclusiveness, charity, openness, concession, and freedom.

The tool in Appendix 3 will help you assess the leaders in your organization as to how poisonous and divisive they are, and how much healing and harmony they inject into the organization.

Part 6:
The Pragmatics

When you do things from your soul, you feel a river moving in you, a joy.

— Rumi

— 8 —

What are the conditions and standards for meaningful, humanizing work?

Walter Lippmann once suggested that the requirements of democracy are great, but the capabilities for making it work are low. John Dewey countered that point of view by arguing that through debate, discussion, and dialogue, a society is capable of achieving a constructive, democratic culture. The same argument could be applied to creating an organizational soul: the requirements are high, the capabilities are low, but productive dialogue can give it a chance of growing.

Pragmatically, the first question to ask is this: What are the conditions and standards required for meaningful, humanizing work? Eight conditions are required to create an organizational soul. They are cultural conditions or factors, not individual leader behaviors described in the previous section. It is always necessary to diagnose whether the lack of organizational soul is an individual problem, or a cultural problem. This section deals with eight cultural factors:

1. Openness
2. Effort
3. Clarity
4. Fairness

5. Innovation
6. Integrity
7. Interdependence
8. Quality

Openness

One of the conditions required to create organizational soul is **openness** to feedback. In order for real change to take place, some individuals and organizations need a shock to their system. Don't worry. I'm not advocating for electroshock therapy (although sometimes I think I ought to have suggested it for some particularly arrogant and abusive managers I have known over the years). The shock comes from fully acknowledging and owning the gaps between how we perceive ourselves and the ways in which we are perceived by others.

Imaginations run wild in organizational leaders. After years of pampering, promotions, and prosperity, many leaders develop inflated opinions of themselves. As one wise friend observed, they start inhaling their own PR. Egos grow so large, they can't be checked at the door. A whole room is needed to accommodate their needs. Leaders who have gaps between their goals and their capabilities, between their résumés and their actual achievements or between the standards for a soulful organization and their day-to-day behaviors are shocked to their core when someone confronts them. Unless, of course, they have developed defense mechanisms that never let the truth penetrate, or they have acquired the habit of turning any bad news right back at the sender, like a reflex reaction. Their mantra is *I will let no news into my psyche that will puncture the inflated image I have of myself.* There is no shock to these leaders, because they have constructed a fortress of buffers that enable them to deny reality. And, thus, there is no change.

In a soulful culture, leaders are open, honest, and direct. They give constructive feedback, but they also receive it graciously and gratefully. Soulful leaders are brutally honest about the facts. They seek out evidence. They are hungry for information that can help them grow. They have an innate sense of shame for not being as helpful to people as they would like to be. They assume responsibility for their actions and for creating positive experiences for others.

Like individuals, organizations also need to be open to hearing things that might shock their organizational operating systems. The best way to provide feedback to organizations is to appoint, legitimize, and encourage a Soul Committee to point out the gaps between stated values and norms and identify the day-to-day organizational behaviors that occur repetitively. One responsibility of the Soul Committee should be to conduct biannual culture audits on desired and required norms that have been identified and endorsed by members of the community. By sharing the results of the audits with the entire organization, leadership sends a message that these norms and values are important, and reinforces expectations about day-to-day behaviors. If the organization's leaders are not willing to seek out and consider feedback that will unsettle or shock them, there is very little chance that the changes will be sustained in an organization, much less that it will be able to create organizational soul.

Effort

One of the factors necessary to create organizational soul is *effort*—specifically the willingness to make efforts to change. Change takes work. If people are not willing to put in the work, there is very little chance of turning a random spark into a roaring flame. As with individuals, organizations don't start with a soul—*they build one.* Soul building is not only the most important thing we can do as individuals and organizations, it is also the most difficult. There are always a thousand reasons to focus on something else. There are always competing pressures for our time. There are always excuses to put it off for another day. With very little effort, however, we can get caught up in the flow of our daily routines, and *whoosh.* Our soul has slipped away.

Effort also means being conscious of what we are doing. It means observing our own personal behavior and organizational behavior with impartial objectivity. Since we tend to be polite and preferential, it's easy to pretend that we are making effort, when we are really not. Making an effort means staying alert to the ways our behaviors impact others and the ways we work together to create a soulful community.

To sustain the effort to develop an organizational soul, people must see the need to make the effort and *want to make the effort.* This work is not easy. There are always setbacks. We get disappointed when we don't make the progress we had hoped for. The real opportunities, however, come out of the setbacks and disappointments. It is during these setbacks that we have to look deep inside and renew our commitment to grow.

With shock and effort, transformational change can occur. With defensiveness and laziness, we can be sure to continue in the same old ways that led us to this point in time.

Clarity

Another condition required to create organizational soul is *clarity.* Clarity is achieved through a systematic and deductive strategic planning process. Leaders must take responsibility for creating a strategic plan, cascading it through the organization, and changing it dynamically as marketplace conditions change. Here are the standards by which you can measure those conditions:

- The vision is clear.
- The values are clear.
- The mission is clear.

- The goals are clear.
- The objectives are clear.
- The strategies are clear.
- Individual roles, responsibilities, and decision "rights" are clear.

A vision is a picture of the ideal end state. It is the desired outcome of all organizational effort. A vision should be inspiring, mobilizing, and energizing. "Achieving $10 billion in revenues" does not make people want to come to work everyday. "Connecting civilizations" is a vision that instills passion throughout the organization. It answers the question *Why am I doing this?* In organizations in which people believe in the vision, everyone gets up every morning with passion flowing through their veins. Even on Monday.

Values serve as the anchors for decision making. They define what's most important in the work environment. Values are the starting point for creating norms of our own choosing. Intelligent organizations use the term "I^3Q" to represent a set of four values: Interdependence, Integrity, Innovation, and Quality. As the corporate and not-for-profit leaders pointed out in Chapter 3, when hard decisions have to be made, having well-defined values helps leaders differentiate among alternatives by the extent to which each option satisfies the values.

Effective organizations have from 3 to 7 values that guide organizational behaviors. Choosing which values are most important requires a soul-searching experience that can't be done superficially, cavalierly, or unilaterally. Here is a partial list of values that organizations have chosen as inspirational and aspirational guideposts.

VALUE GUIDEPOSTS

- Achievement
- Boldness
- Communication
- Decisiveness
- Energy
- Fairness
- Growth
- Health
- Impact
- Justice
- Knowledge
- Laughter
- Measurement
- Openness
- Play
- Quality
- Respect
- Safety
- Trust
- Unity
- Winning

When you make your own list of company values, you might not want to include some of the examples listed above. Just make sure you make a conscious decision about the values that characterize *your* organization. The point is that values take shape and get institutionalized with or without leadership involvement. They either come alive insidiously, or come alive by design. When employees feel that they have a voice in the values the organization adopts, it is more likely that the values will serve as true guideposts through our organizational growth and turmoil.

Each value needs to be translated into a set of desired and required norms. For example, the employees might decide that those norms are the best set of behavioral indicators for a high level of respect in the organization:

We value differences.
We are inclusive.
We treat people with dignity.
We criticize in private and praise in public.
We are harder on ourselves than we are on others.

These norms answer two questions:

What does respect look like in our organization?

How would we know when we had it?

Appendix 4 contains a tool for measuring desired behaviors for each of the conditional factors discussed in this section.

The Mission

A mission statement describes the nature of the work. It answers this question: What do we do for whom? A good mission statement provides strategic direction for 3 to 5 years. "Becoming a leading provider of services" is not an effective mission statement. Not only is it too abstract, but it is a goal of companies and thousands of organizations.

Let's use the mission statement of the Visiting Nurses Association of Somerset Hills as an example. It identifies the target audience and the specific services it offers:

> To provide individuals and families with comprehensive, high-quality, cost-effective home and community health-care services, regardless of the ability to pay, using partnerships where appropriate.

A good mission statement enables all members of the organization to assess how well their work contributes to the mission. Without a well-defined mission, it is impossible to align the organization.

Goals

Goals are statements about the direction the organization intends to take for the next 1 to 3 years. They represent the area of focus for the organization. Most goals fall under the following categories:

- People (example: To provide developmental opportunities for all stakeholders)
- Process (example: To increase organizational efficiency and effectiveness)
- Product (example: To create leading-edge products for our customers)
- Program (example: To provide high-quality programs for our customers)
- Technology (example: To enable communications, teamwork, and decision making)
- Organization (example: To align the culture with the strategy)
- Finance (example: To grow our profits and reserves)

You will notice that the examples for each of these goals are not specific or measurable, nor are they meant to be. Goals should simply provide directional guidance and help you ascertain that you are taking into account all the critical elements of high-performing organizations.

Objectives provide the measures of success for any given year. Objectives should be crafted to satisfy A-SMART criteria:

- Aligned
- Specific
- Measurable
- Achievable
- Results-oriented
- Time-bound

I've reviewed thousands of individual and organizational objectives over the years, and my experience is that most objectives fail to meet all of the A-SMART criteria. Most commonly, they tend to be activity-based instead of results-oriented and time-bound objectives. Many are not aligned with organizational goals or are entirely unrealistic. When people are confused about what they are supposed to achieve and do not know precisely how their work fits with the organizational strategy, they are unlikely to have much energy for creating organizational soul.

Only when individual and organizational objectives are clear does it make sense to develop the best strategies for achieving the objectives. In soulful organizations, through a series of meaningful conversations, managers come to agreement about the objectives for the year (*what* results are expected) and then provide a great deal of latitude about the strategies for achieving those results (*how* the work gets done). The degree of latitude, of course, depends upon the commitment and capabilities of the person who is responsible for the results. People with low commitment and/or low capabilities might require more direction and support. People with high commitment and high capabilities might only need delegation and minimal coaching. In soulful organizations, managers make good judgments about commitment, capability, and the required levels of direction and support. In soulless organizations, they don't.

The final element of clarity is having clearly defined roles, rights, and responsibilities. The flash point normally occurs around decision rights. In organizations in which employees experience soul-draining ambiguity, these questions usually arise:

- I have all these responsibilities, but how much authority do I have?

- Who has to approve this decision?
- Who is really accountable for this action?
- Am I just providing input, or am I really responsible?
- Should I be acting as a consultant, or am I accountable for the results?

The likelihood of these questions being raised is reduced in organizations that have taken pains to start with the vision, values, mission, goals, and objectives. If any of those elements are fuzzy, there is much greater chance that people will be asking themselves these kinds of questions.

The soul of this activity resides in the thoughtfulness and reflection with which these words are crafted. The soul is in the dialogue and discussion, not in the perfunctory exercise of putting words on paper that have little meaning to most employees in the organization.

The soul is in the engagement and involvement of all employees in creating clear and meaningful statements of vision, values, mission, goals, and objectives.

Fairness

Another conditional factor required to create organizational soul is fairness. Fairness is demonstrated through accurate and objective performance, development, and succession planning processes. Leadership must own these processes so critical to the business. Here are the standards by which you can measure those conditions:

First Quarter

- All employees have A-SMART objectives and development plans in the first month of the performance year.

- All employees have engaged in productive dialogue with their supervisor about performance and development objectives, and have agreed to them.

- Nominated candidates for targeted jobs have potential and readiness ratings for those jobs.

- All employees have had career-development discussions with their supervisor.

- Calibration meetings have been held to ensure accuracy of performance and potential ratings.

- Performance ratings are based on leadership and results.

- Potential ratings are based on learning agility, experience, and motivation.

Second Quarter

- All employees engage in meaningful conversations about progress on performance and development objectives.

- Succession charts are developed for all mission-critical positions.

- Facilitated meetings are held with leadership teams to review succession charts.

Third Quarter

- Strategic plans are clarified for the next 3 years.

- Business plans are detailed for the following year.

- Leaders are aligned behind the strategy and business plan.

- Critical positions are identified for successful implementation of the strategy and business plans.

- Capability requirements are identified for each position.
- Each employee has a meeting with his or her supervisor to discuss potential ratings.
- All employees are clear about their career goals, the required capabilities to achieve those goals, the perceptions others have about their capabilities, and the standards for their targeted jobs.

Fourth Quarter

- All employees engage in meaningful conversations with their employer about their performance (what they achieved and how they achieved it) and about their development.
- Compensation plans are based on performance and development as discussed during review sessions.
- Complete and accurate information is contained in all employee files.

Performance and Succession programs are deployed through a consistent global framework that:

- Is consistent with and supports organizational values
- Reinforces a **pay for performance** culture; drives the organization toward continued **differentiation**
- Is focused on enabling the **achievement of strategic plans and annual business plans**
- Requires equal **ownership and accountability** from everyone
- Is **simple and transparent**

- **Engages, encourages, and motivates** employees to work toward their highest level of performance

- Holds managers accountable, and assesses managers for their **people-development skills**—specifically **providing the feedback, direction, and support needed for development**, in order to help employees achieve their career and performance aspirations

- Accelerates and facilitates the **development and deployment** of key talent

Fairness exists in an organization when there are clear guidelines for rating results and leadership. The chart below provides differential distinctions for rating business results, leadership, and people development.

RATING BUSINESS RESULTS, LEADERSHIP, AND STAFF DEVELOPMENT

Business Results			
Does not meet	**Partially meets**	**Fully meets**	**Exceeds**
Does not deliver results on majority of agreed-upon financial and non-financial goals	Inconsistently delivers results on agreed-upon financial and non-financial goals	Delivers results on majority of and occasionally surpasses agreed-upon financial and non-financial goals	Delivers results that substantially exceed all agreed-upon financial and non-financial goals

(continued)

Leadership			
Does not meet	**Partially meets**	**Fully meets**	**Exceeds**
Does not demonstrate competencies in a positive manner. Exhibits derailing behaviors.	Inconsistently demonstrates competencies. Understands the need for development and is taking steps to improve.	Uses competencies to achieve objectives Has a positive impact by demonstrating the competencies	Inspires others by role modeling the competencies Has positive broad organizational impact by demonstrating the competencies
People Development			
Does not meet	**Partially meets**	**Fully meets**	**Exceeds**
Does not deliver results on majority of agreed-upon people-development goals	Inconsistently delivers results on agreed-upon people-development goals	Delivers results on majority of and occasionally surpasses agreed-upon people-development goals	Delivers results that substantially exceed all agreed-upon people-development goals

Fairness exists in an organization when managers engage in meaningful conversations with their employees about performance and development. While each conversation is tailored to an employee's particular situation, there is a common template managers use to guide the conversation. (Examples of templates for three critical conversations can be found in Appendix 5.)

Fairness exists in an organization when each employee has a development plan that sets reasonable expectations, as well as support. Development planning has three major milestones during the year:

1. The initial meeting to set up the development plan and schedule activities at the beginning of the year (with the manager).

2. A discussion with the manager regarding progress (at mid-year).

3. A status completion update (at year end). It is also expected that development activities and developmental feedback occur continually throughout the year.

Fairness in performance and development requires leaders to measure management effectiveness in coaching and feedback. Direct reports should provide feedback regarding their manager's performance during the "stakeholder feedback" process, which is used as input by their manager's manager when preparing the year-end assessment for their manager.

Fairness requires the organization to set up a succession planning process that enables managers to assess the performance, potential, and readiness of employees to succeed in target positions. The succession planning process enables leaders to assess bench strength and to make informed investment decisions regarding deployment and development.

Innovation

"A person flattened by conformity stays down for good."

— Thomas Watson

One of the conditional factors required to create organizational soul is **innovation.** Soul can be defined as a creative force that guides our actions. Therefore, soul and innovation are inextricably linked. In an innovative organization, there is passion, creativity, and an endless pursuit of possibility. People are making connections, building on each other's ideas, and seeking out new sources of gain. There is a continuous generation of new ideas. These are the signposts of an innovative culture.

Innovation requires thinking. In a thinking organization, there is reflection and contemplation. There is no conflict between ideation and action. People understand that generating ideas is not a random activity, but is aligned with the mission. Interdependent processing is valued.

Integrity

One of the conditional factors required to create organizational soul is **integrity.** Most organizations include integrity in their value statements, but few actually make serious attempts to measure it. Four key components of integrity are:

- Dependability (people do what they say they will do)
- Honesty (people say what they have done)
- Genuineness (people say what they believe)
- Consciousness (people are aware of what they do)

The primary function of dependability is to **build trust.** If there is a lack of trust in the organization, it is nearly impossible to engage in healthy conflict, to deepen commitment, to maximize ownership, or to achieve results. If team members can count on other members to deliver on their promises, there is less micro-managing and cynicism in the organization. Dependability, therefore, is an essential component of integrity, and trust is the primary function of dependability.

The primary function of honesty is to **build confidence.** If people are perceived as being dishonest, there is a lack of confidence is what members of an organization hear in conversations and conferences or see in memos and messages. In a high-integrity organization, there is a great deal of transparency and there are few secrets. Saying what you have done (honesty) means taking appropriate credit for what goes right and accepting appropriate responsibility for what goes wrong. When people take too little or too much credit and/or not enough responsibility, integrity is tarnished. Honesty, therefore, is an essential component of integrity, and confidence is the primary function of honesty.

The primary function of **genuineness** is to build and strengthen the organization's **belief in possibilities.** When people in the organization are genuine, there is a sense that what is being said can be believed. There is no pandering and spin that characterizes so much of political discourse. Organizations that encourage and promote genuine conversations are rarely described as political. Genuineness, therefore, is an essential component of integrity, and building belief is the primary function of genuineness.

The primary function of **consciousness** is to grow. When people are conscious, they are focused, awake and aware of what they are doing in the moment, as well as aware of how their behavior affects others. Consciousness means being alert to environmental conditions, community prosperity, and organizational productivity. In a conscious organization, leaders are socially responsible and environmentally sensitive. Consciousness, therefore, is an essential component of integrity, and growth (individual, organizational, and community) is the primary function of consciousness.

Dependability, honesty, genuineness, and consciousness are considered to be critical ingredients in a high-integrity organization. If integrity is an essential element of organizational soul, then the question becomes "How do you measure integrity?" As I mentioned earlier, the most effective process is to establish a Soul Committee whose sole purpose is to identify the gaps between what we say and what we do, and what we do and what we say. The Soul Committee should be officially sanctioned by the executive committee to report on the components of a high-integrity organization (dependability, genuineness, honesty, and consciousness) as well as the functions (trust, confidence, belief, and growth.)

Interdependence

One of the conditional factors required to create organizational soul is **interdependent thinking.** Most organizations are competitive and independent. This description wouldn't be so bad if it applied to the external marketplace, but I'm describing the internal organization. For example, it is not unusual for sales and engineering to operate competitively and independently. Both are vying for scarce resources, and both view the other with suspicion. An engineer might say, "Don't tell me what the customer wants. I know this is the product we need to develop." A sales person might say, "We could sell a lot more of these if engineering would just give us a decent product."

In interdependent organizations, everyone looks for ways to help others succeed. Customer-facing people seek to understand customer needs and create solutions that address those needs. Departments work cross-functionally to develop the best possible solutions. There is not only open communication and sharing, but people are cooperative and collaborative as well. Internal and external customers consistently give high ratings on the scale below to the people with whom they interface:

5: Trusted advisor (most important)
4: Value-added partner
3: Solutions provider
2: Preferred services provider
1: Product or service pusher (least important)

A **trusted advisor** is one of the first people you call when you have an issue that needs to be resolved. This is a person who has the perspective, experience, and capabilities that will help you grow. A **value-added partner** is someone who can enter into your conversation and contribute novel and constructive ideas. A **solutions provider** is someone who understands your needs and has a repertoire of responses to help you with your problem. A **services provider** is someone with whom you have worked in the past who has the capabilities to help you solve your problems. This person is a dependable and reliable resource for you. A **product or service pusher** simply wants you to buy what they are selling independent of your needs. Unfortunately, most customer satisfaction surveys measure the extent to which you provide services. There is rarely any mention of solutions, partnerships, or trusted relationships.

Interdependent organizations usually have collaboration communities in which people work together to continually improve existing processes or create new sources of gain. Collaboration communities can consist of people who are interested in the same ideas or who practice similar professions. The purpose of collaboration communities is to create thinking environments that encourage people to stretch their horizons, learn new skills, and deepen their relationships. Collaboration communities provide a forum for the exchange of ideas and perspectives. The most-effective communities have diverse points of view, diverse thinking/learning styles, and diverse experiences. The healthy interchange of ideas stimulates deep dialogue and generates exciting new ideas. There is a vibrant energy in these communities.

Quality

One of the conditional factors required to create organizational soul is a **quality mindset.** There are high demands for excellence. There is real passion in the organization to meet commitments in accordance with requirements and time frames. Most organizations only apply this quality mindset to product development. **Six sigma** programs and **process excellence** programs are primarily dedicated to improving product quality. In soulful organizations, there are high standards for everything we do. The grid on the following page presents one way to illustrate where leaders should look for opportunities to make qualitative improvement.

	Leadership	Marketing and Sales	Human, Information, and Financial Resources	Technology	Production, Manufacturing, and/or Operations
Make policy decisions					
Make executive policy decisions					
Manage implementation					
Supervise delivery or implementation					
Deliver or implement					

This matrix, adapted from Carkhuff's grid illustrating the components of an organization, can be used as a jumping-off point for further discussion about continuous improvement. Leaders can ask such questions as:

How effective are managers at setting goals for marketing and sales?

What can we do to improve that process?

How well are our executives measuring our return on investment in technology?

Organizational soul can only come from the culture you create within the organization: a culture of Openness, Effort, Clarity, Fairness, Innovation, Integrity, Interdependence, and Quality.

Part 7:

The Present

Art is a microscope which the artist fixes on the secrets of his soul, and shows to people these secrets which are common to all.

— Leo Tolstoy

— 9 —

Where are we today?
And where do we go from here?

I believe our purpose in life is to develop our souls as individuals and as organizations. As individuals, we have been given the gift of possibility—the opportunity to take a spark of life and grow it into something useful. As organizations, the same possibility exists. In each moment, day-to-day, we either make a difference or we don't.

In the Introduction, I mentioned some early heroes of the 21st century: Paul Farmer, Jeffrey Sachs, Lucy Caulkins, Bob Carkhuff, Betsey Hall, and Julie Meek. Some of these names are familiar to you, and some you have probably never heard of. If you don't know them, Google them as fast as you can. They are all worth knowing.

But we can't rely on the heroes to drag us out of the mess we have created for ourselves. Each one of us needs to step up in each moment and lead. It is not acceptable to detract. It is not enough to observe. We all need to participate, contribute, and lead to the best of our ability. We need to develop our own souls, and create souls in the organizations in which we work. Each of us needs to take responsibility to create peace and harmony in each moment—day after day.

The stories I shared in this book illustrate what an organization can achieve if it develops *organizational soul*. These results clearly exceed what soulless organizations achieve. More importantly, they are sustainable.

In this book, I've outlined the principles of soulful organizations and discussed the indicators of *soulful* and *soulless* organizations. I have detailed the conditions for creating organizational soul, and shared success stories of people who have worked to create soulful organizations.

So where do we go from here? Up the scales, together. We can only be successful if we think interdependently, deductively, and systematically. My best wishes for creating a soul that will sustain you and results that will reward you.

Appendix

Appendix 1: A Tool for Measuring Organizational Soul *Health*

The items on this short assessment represent what a soulful organization looks like. It is a list of the norms you would find in a healthy, innovative, productive environment. As such, the tool serves two purposes: 1) to educate people on the elements of organizational soul, and 2) to establish a baseline to assess where you are and where you want to be. After working together to craft a constructive corporate culture, people in your organization should be able to say that they see these behaviors demonstrated every day.

Check all the items that describe your current organization:

- ❏ We trust each other.
- ❏ We feel empowered.
- ❏ We engage in meaningful dialogue.
- ❏ There is a high level of reflection on critical issues.
- ❏ We engage in healthy conflict.
- ❏ We are passionate about a higher purpose.
- ❏ There is a high level of creative energy.
- ❏ We are inclusive.
- ❏ We are always learning.
- ❏ We are caring and compassionate.
- ❏ There is a high level of integrity.
- ❏ We value and respect differences.
- ❏ We are genuine.

- ❏ We are brutally honest about the facts of our situation.
- ❏ We encourage growth and well-being.
- ❏ We seek ways to help each other succeed. We collaborate.
- ❏ We are committed to the organization.
- ❏ We hold each other accountable.
- ❏ We drive for results.
- ❏ We are open, honest, and direct.

Score 5 points for each item you check that is representative of your organization, and add up the points to get a total score. 100% represents a perfect score.

Appendix 2: A Tool for Measuring Organizational Soul *Sickness*

Use this tool to diagnose how healthy the organization is. It lists ten warning signs that the culture is in real trouble. If these behaviors constitute a somewhat accurate description of your organization, you can be sure that there is little motivation, innovation, productivity, or passion. A majority of responses in any of three "Agree" categories indicates the severity of the crisis. Use the results of this survey to help you determine the requirements for the intervention.

	Strongly disagree	Disagree	Somewhat agree	Agree	Strongly agree
1. People look tired.	❏	❏	❏	❏	❏
2. Key people are leaving.	❏	❏	❏	❏	❏
3. Conversations are disingenuous.	❏	❏	❏	❏	❏
4. If there is a mistake, the solution is to cover it up.	❏	❏	❏	❏	❏
5. There is a short-term focus.	❏	❏	❏	❏	❏
6. The organization doesn't learn.	❏	❏	❏	❏	❏
7. Training is focused on weaknesses.	❏	❏	❏	❏	❏
8. Managers act unilaterally.	❏	❏	❏	❏	❏
9. The organization violates the environment.	❏	❏	❏	❏	❏
10. Critics get all the attention.	❏	❏	❏	❏	❏

Appendix 3: A Leadership Assessment Tool

This tool will help you determine the extent to which your organization's leadership will either enable or retard your efforts to create a healthy organizational soul. Please indicate where you believe your organization's leaders fall in each of the seven descriptors. Add the number of checkmarks in each column. Low totals suggest that any culture change effort is likely to fail. High totals suggest that you have good reason to believe that your efforts will be successful.

Culture change requires strong leadership support and role modeling, as well as a reward system that reinforces desired behaviors. Without leadership role modeling, however, it is impossible to achieve sustainable change.

Soulless Leaders	1	2	3	4	5	Soulful Leaders
Arrogant	❏	❏	❏	❏	❏	Humble
Not inquiring	❏	❏	❏	❏	❏	Curious
Exclusive	❏	❏	❏	❏	❏	Inclusive
Greedy	❏	❏	❏	❏	❏	Charitable
Condescending	❏	❏	❏	❏	❏	Concessionary
Closed	❏	❏	❏	❏	❏	Open
Controlling	❏	❏	❏	❏	❏	Freeing

Appendix 4: A Tool for Assessing Soulful Conditions

This tool enables you to measure how well you are doing at creating organizational soul. It should be administered at the beginning of a culture change effort, and every year thereafter.

Please indicate the extent to which you agree or disagree with each of the following descriptors as representative of your organizational culture.

Pay special attention to the checkmarks in the "Strongly disagree" and "Disagree" columns, because they point to deficiencies. Use the results to communicate to the organization its strengths and weaknesses, and use them to shape its focus for the future. Task forces should be formed to leverage strengths and to work on areas of concern.

Required Conditions	Strongly disagree	Disagree	Somewhat agree	Agree	Strongly agree
OPENNESS					
We give constructive feedback.	❏	❏	❏	❏	❏
We get constructive feedback.	❏	❏	❏	❏	❏
We engage in open, honest, and direct communication.	❏	❏	❏	❏	❏
We share information.	❏	❏	❏	❏	❏
Leaders want to hear the good, the bad, and the ugly.	❏	❏	❏	❏	❏

(continued)

A Tool for Assessing Soulful Conditions (continued)

Required Conditions	Strongly disagree	Disagree	Somewhat agree	Agree	Strongly agree
EFFORT					
We strive diligently to grow.	❏	❏	❏	❏	❏
We work hard.	❏	❏	❏	❏	❏
CLARITY					
The vision is clear.	❏	❏	❏	❏	❏
Our values are clear.	❏	❏	❏	❏	❏
The mission is clear.	❏	❏	❏	❏	❏
Our goals are clear.	❏	❏	❏	❏	❏
Roles, responsibilities, and decision rights are clear.	❏	❏	❏	❏	❏
FAIRNESS					
We know where we stand.	❏	❏	❏	❏	❏
Rewards are based on merit.	❏	❏	❏	❏	❏
Compensation is equitable.	❏	❏	❏	❏	❏
INNOVATION					
We take risks.	❏	❏	❏	❏	❏
We learn from our mistakes.	❏	❏	❏	❏	❏
We share ideas.	❏	❏	❏	❏	❏

(continued)

A Tool for Assessing Soulful Conditions (concluded)

Required Conditions	Strongly disagree	Disagree	Somewhat agree	Agree	Strongly agree
INTEGRITY					
We do what we say.	❏	❏	❏	❏	❏
We say what we do.	❏	❏	❏	❏	❏
We are genuine.	❏	❏	❏	❏	❏
INTERDEPENDENCE					
We seek ways to help each other succeed.	❏	❏	❏	❏	❏
We leverage each other's strengths.	❏	❏	❏	❏	❏
QUALITY					
We meet commitments in accordance with requirements.	❏	❏	❏	❏	❏
We strive for excellence.	❏	❏	❏	❏	❏
We continually improve every aspect of our organization.	❏	❏	❏	❏	❏

Note: Please feel free to modify this assessment tool to add norms of your own choosing.

Appendix 5: A Conversation Template for Goal-Setting Sessions

Set the stage.

Purpose. The purpose of this meeting is to agree on your performance objectives for the year (i.e., what you expect to accomplish this year for the business), and to agree on your developmental objectives for the year (i.e., how you plan to use the leadership competencies to improve the ways in which you achieve your objectives).

The employee's input. Last week, I asked you to come prepared to do three things: to discuss your 5 to 7 objectives for the year; review the leadership competencies overview I sent to you; and outline your development plan. Are you ready, willing, and able to discuss those three items on our agenda? Do you have any questions before we begin?

Set objectives.

The *"What."* Let's begin with your performance objectives. What did you write down for your objectives?

The *"How."* Let's talk about how you can accomplish those objectives in a way that is aligned with the leadership competencies. Have you completed your acknowledgement of the leadership competencies? As you noticed, the leadership competencies have been scaled to define progressive levels of mastery on each of the competencies. What connection do you see between using the leadership competency behaviors and achieving business results? Did you have any questions on the competencies and how they are scaled?

The *plan:* Let's agree on what development strategy makes the most sense for you this year.

Set expectations.

Go over the manager's expectations. Let's talk about what I expect from you this year, and what you can expect from me to make sure you are successful in achieving your performance and development goals.

Clearly, I expect you to accomplish what we agreed on today. I also expect you to come to me for help if you need coaching, direction, or support. You can expect me to be accessible to you when needed and possible; to have a conversation with you mid-year to discuss how you are doing on the objectives we set; and to conduct a formal end-of-year evaluation with you.

The employee's expectations. What expectations do you have of me for the upcoming year? What support do you think you will need in order to accomplish these objectives?

Set the tone.

Manager's close. I appreciate your efforts in preparing for this meeting, as well as your candor in discussing your objectives. I feel good about what we have agreed to and I am confident that you will be successful. I will do whatever I can to help you be successful. Do you have any questions or concerns?

Appendix 6. A Conversation Template for a Mid-Year Review

Set the stage.

Purpose. The purpose of this meeting is to discuss how you are doing on the performance and development objectives we set for you at the beginning of the year.

The employee's input. Last week, I asked you to come prepared to discuss your progress on the 5 to 7 objectives for the year and your development plan. Do you have any questions before we begin?

Review objectives.

The *"What."* Let's begin with your performance objectives. How are you doing on your objectives? Do you feel you are where you need to be in order to successfully meet your year-end metric? Are you encountering any obstacles or difficulties?

The *"How."* Let's talk about how you are doing at accomplishing those objectives in a way that is aligned with our global leadership competencies. On which of the competencies do you have a sense of urgency and desire to "move up the scales?" How do you think moving up the scales will help you improve business results? What kind of progress are you making? And how do you see that progress translating into business results?

The *plan.* What progress are you making on your development plan? How are your assignments and experiences helping you to develop your capabilities? What kind of feedback and coaching are you getting? What instructional programs have you been able to take advantage of? What have you found most useful?

Set expectations.

Manager's expectations. Let's talk about how well we are meeting each other's expectations. Are you getting the coaching, direction, and support you need in order to be successful? Have I been accessible enough to you? Which form of communication seems to work best for us: e-mail, voice-mail, or face-to-face meetings? What I expect from you in communicating with me is. . .

The employee's expectations. How am I doing at meeting the expectations you had for me? Do you have any additional expectations or needs at this time?

Set the tone.

Manager's close. I appreciate your efforts in preparing for this meeting, as well as your candor in discussing your objectives. I feel good about your progress and confident that you will be successful. I look forward to our end-of-year discussion. I am hoping we will have a great deal to celebrate about your own development and business results. Do you have any questions or concerns?

Appendix 7. A Conversation Template for an End-of-Year Review

Set the stage.

Purpose. The purpose of this meeting is to evaluate how well you did at achieving the performance and development objectives we set for you at the beginning of the year and that we reviewed mid-year.

The employee's input. Last week, I asked you to come prepared to discuss how you would evaluate your level of achievement on the 5 to 7 objectives for the year, and the extent to which you were able to implement your development plan. Do you have any questions before we begin?

Review objectives.

The *"What."* Let's begin with your performance objectives. To what extent did you achieve your objectives? On the 4-point scale of Does not Meet, Partially Meets, Fully Meets, and Exceeds, how did you rate yourself on each objective? What do you believe were the biggest reasons for your success or lack of success? What did you learn?

The *"How."* Let's talk about how you were able to use the global leadership competencies to achieve your performance objectives. In our goal-setting meeting, you mentioned that you had a sense of urgency and desire to move up the scales on the competencies of ___ and ___. What kind of progress did you make? How did you see that progress translate into business results?

The *Plan.* To what extent were you able to implement your development plan? How did your assignments and experiences help you to develop your capabilities? What kind of feedback and coaching did you get that was helpful? What instructional programs were you able to take advantage of? What have you found most useful? What did you learn?

Set expectations.

Manager's expectations. Let's talk about how well we met each other's expectations. Did you get the coaching, direction, and support you needed to be successful? Was I accessible enough to you? Which form of communication worked best for us: e-mail, voice-mail, or face-to-face meetings? From my point of view. . .

The employee's expectations. How well did I meet the expectations you had for me? Do you have any additional expectations or needs at this time?

Set the tone.

Manager's close. I appreciate your efforts in preparing for this meeting, as well as your candor in discussing your objectives. I feel good about your contribution to the business and the impact you are making in the organization through your leadership competency role modeling. I am confident that you will be successful in achieving your career objectives, based on the results you achieved this year and the way in which you achieved them. I look forward to working with you next year. Do you have any questions or concerns about anything we discussed? Do you agree with the ratings I gave you for both performance and development?

About the Author

Richard Bellingham is an organizational psychologist with more than 30 years of experience in executive coaching, strategic planning, leadership development, and organizational learning in high-tech, telecommunications, health care, financial, and professional service firms. The CEO of Iobility, a New Jersey-based consulting group, he has helped organizations in Asia, Europe, and Latin America, as well as leaders in U.S. businesses large and small, and executives in more than half of this country's Fortune 100 companies.

Prior to opening his own consulting firm, Rick held executive positions at Parametric Technology, Genzyme, and Northern Telecom, and has provided pro bono services at the board level to several not-for-profit social-service organizations for the past 25 years.

Rick served as an adjunct faculty member at Harvard University, where he co-founded the Forum for Intelligent Organizations, and has taught culture change, health-care management, and leadership development at several U.S. universities. He has published articles in peer-reviewed journals, and is the author of 15 books on leadership, culture, and HR strategy. Titles include *The Leadership Lexicon, Ethical Leadership, Leadership Myths and Realities, HR Optimization, Corporate Culture Change,* and *Virtual Teams.*

He and his wife of 39 years, a special education teacher, have two daughters.

www.ingramcontent.com/pod-product-compliance
Lightning Source LLC
Chambersburg PA
CBHW032331210326
41518CB00041B/2065